This Belongs to the One and Only Jessica Marie Wright

Be Still and Know that I am God!!!

Praise be to God!!!

Register This New Book

Benefits of Registering*

- ✓ FREE **replacements** of lost or damaged books
- ✓ FREE **audiobook** – *Pilgrim's Progress*, audiobook edition
- ✓ FREE information about new titles and other **freebies**

www.anekopress.com/new-book-registration

*See our website for requirements and limitations.

The Resurrection of the Dead, and Eternal Judgment

Behold, I show you a mystery; we shall not all sleep, but we shall all be changed, in a moment, in the twinkling of an eye, at the last trump: for the trumpet shall sound, and the dead shall be raised incorruptible, and we shall be changed.
– 1 Corinthians 15:51-52

Marvel not at this: for the hour is coming, in the which all that are in the graves shall hear his voice, and shall come forth; they that have done good, unto the resurrection of life; and they that have done evil, unto the resurrection of damnation.
– John 5:28-29

The
Resurrection
of the Dead,
and Eternal
Judgment

Or

The Truth of the Resurrection of the Bodies,
Both of Good and Bad at the Last Day:
Asserted and Proved by God's Word.

John Bunyan,

A Servant of the Lord's Christ

We love hearing from our readers. Please contact us at www.anekopress.com/questions-comments with any questions, comments, or suggestions.

The Resurrection of the Dead, and Eternal Judgment
© 2022 by Aneko Press
All rights reserved. First edition 1665.
Revisions copyright 2022.

Scripture quotations from The Authorized (King James) Version. Rights in the Authorized Version in the United Kingdom are vested in the Crown. Reproduced by permission of the Crown's patentee, Cambridge University Press.

Cover Design: J. Martin
Editor: Paul Miller

Aneko Press

www.anekopress.com
Aneko Press, Life Sentence Publishing, and our logos are trademarks of
Life Sentence Publishing, Inc.
203 E. Birch Street
P.O. Box 652
Abbotsford, WI 54405
RELIGION / Christian Theology / Eschatology
Paperback ISBN: 978-1-62245-809-7
eBook ISBN: 978-1-62245-810-3
10 9 8 7 6 5 4 3 2
Available where books are sold

Contents

Message by the Editor

Judging from the style in which it is written, this very important work was probably one of the first books composed by Bunyan. The form in which it is prepared, with minute divisions to assist the memory, along with its conversational language, indicates that it was first intended for the pulpit and then enlarged to form a more complete writing.

A good copy of what appears to be the first edition is in the British Museum. Doe, in his catalogue of all of Mr. Bunyan's books, appended to the *Heavenly Footman*, 1690, states that "*The resurrection of the Dead, and eternal Judgment by John Bunyan, a servant of the Lord's Christ*, was first published in 1665."

The resurrection of the body is a subject of universal and deep importance. It defies our reasoning powers while it exalts our ideas of the divine omnipotence. With God, all things revealed in His Word are not only possible, but are certain of accomplishment. The bodies of the saints, which are a part of the Redeemer's purchase, will be raised in heavenly and wondrous perfection, similar to the Savior's glorious body. That body, when transfigured, *did shine as the sun, and his raiment was white as the light* (Matthew 17:2). That body, which after His resurrection could be touched, but which could appear and disappear to human eyes, as in a closed room filled with His disciples (John 20:19, 26). He could be touched, yet could vanish away, as on the road to Emmaus (Luke 24:31). He could eat with them on the seashore (John 21:9, 15), and could ascend to heaven from the mount (Acts 1:9).

Thus it was foretold by the prophet and reiterated by the apostle: *Eye hath not seen, nor ear heard, neither have entered into the heart of man, the things which God hath prepared for them that love him* (1 Corinthians 2:9; see also Isaiah 64:4). Not one atom of our dust can be lost. This is a bright and glorious anticipation to the saints, but how somber and dreadful a thought it is to those who die without hope! Among Christians, it is common to think and talk of the happiness of the spirits of the just made perfect (Hebrews 12:23), but sadly, how seldom we think or speak of the perfect bliss of our whole nature: body, soul, and spirit – incorruptible, undefiled, and glorified – every part equally the object of the Savior's purchase and of His care.

This writing, which will be ever new and ever important, was especially required in Bunyan's early days. Under the protectorate, the minds of men, which had been kept in slavery, became suddenly emancipated from human creeds and rituals of public worship. The personal attention of everyone was then directed to the Bible. The Lord's Day was observed, and men were chosen as ministers because of their deep and humble piety rather than based upon important people they knew. Tens of thousands became happy in a personal knowledge of divine truth.

At such a period, it must have happened that some evil spirits would exalt themselves, and that even some serious inquirers would draw strange conclusions from a misconception of divine truth and would dimly see *men as trees walking* (Mark 8:24). Among these there appeared teachers who, unable to comprehend how that body which had gone to dust, or in some cases had been reduced by fire to its primary elements and had been dispersed to the winds or waves, could be again produced. They revived an ancient error that the new birth was the only resurrection from death, and consequently, that to those who were born again, the resurrection was passed.

The individuals who expressed these opinions do not appear to have been associated together as a sect or a church. The greater number were insultingly called "ranters," and some were called "quakers." It is very probable that this writing was intended as an antidote to these delusions. We must not conclude from the opinions of a few unworthy individuals, who justly deserved censure, that Bunyan meant to reflect upon the Society of Friends. This treatise was printed in 1665, but it was not until 1675 that the Quakers' rules of discipline were first published, and they from that time as a sect have been, in a high degree, conformable to the morality and heavenly influences of the gospel.

But even before this, Fox, Crisp, Penn, Barclay, and others, who afterward formed the Society of Friends, had declared their full belief in this doctrine:

- "The resurrection of the just and unjust – the last judgment – heaven and hell as future rewards – we believe and confess."

- "We believe the holy manhood of Christ to be in heavenly glory."

- "We acknowledge a resurrection in order to eternal recompence, and rest contented with that body that it will please God to give us."

- "We do firmly believe that besides the resurrection of the soul from the death of sin, to a life of righteousness while here, there will be a resurrection

of the dead hereafter, and that we must all appear
before the judgment seat of Christ."

Robert Barclay, in his catechism of 1673, clearly asserts Bunyan's
own ideas of the resurrection. But in the face of these, and a
thousand similar declarations, the most blatant attacks were
asserted by a fanatic clergyman, Alexander Ross, in his *View
of all Religions*:

The Ranters are a sect of beasts that neither divide the hoof
nor chew the cud; that is to say, they are very unclean ones.
They, like the Quakers, oppose forms and order (the form and
order of the *Book of Common Prayer*). To examine this mon-
ster: (1) They hold that God, demons, angels, heaven, and hell
are fictions. (2) That Moses, John the Baptist, and Christ were
impostors. (3) That preaching and praying is lying. (1696, p. 273)

Such wild slanders were uttered occasionally against all
Dissenters until a much later period. It is good that they are
now better known and the truths of Christianity are more
appreciated. I have been careful to mention this subject so that
it is not thought that Bunyan had in any degree manifested
the spirit of those who, even to the present day, misrepresent
the opinions of the Quakers. This may be occasioned by their
distinctive belief that the work of the ministry is purely a labor
of love and should not be performed for hire. This belief comes
from the command of Christ to His disciples: *Freely ye have
received, freely give* (Matthew 10:8). This, however, is no reason
that they should be misrepresented and slandered as to their
general views of divine truth.

John Bunyan, at all times solemn and impactful, is especially serious and penetrating in this writing. The dead will
arise involuntarily and irresistibly. Conscience, uncontrolled,
must testify all the truth to the condemnation of the soul and
body, unless cleansed from sin by faith in the Redeemer and the
sacred influences of the Holy Spirit. The books will be opened,

and every thought, word, and action will be seen inscribed in characters legible to all. Every soul will be able to read and clearly understand those mysterious books – God's omniscient, penetrating, and universal sight of all things from the creation of the world to the final consummation – and He has perfect remembrance of all that He saw.

There is then no refuge, no escape. The word "depart" compels obedience (Psalm 6:8; Matthew 7:23; 25:41), and the sinner plunges into eternal woe! Oh, that the living may lay these dreadful realities to heart and fly for refuge to the arms of the Redeemer. He only is able, He alone is willing to save to the uttermost all who come unto God by Him (Hebrews 7:25). Those who find in Him a refuge from the storms of life will hear His voice irresistibly compelling them to heaven: *Come, ye blessed of my Father, inherit the kingdom prepared for you from the foundation of the world* (Matthew 25:34).

> Oh, glorious hour! Oh, blessed abode!
> I will be like and near my God!
> And flesh and sin no more control
> The sacred pleasures of the soul.[1]

May the divine blessing abundantly attend the reading of these dreadful or joyful realities.

—George Offor

---

1   This is from a hymn by Isaac Watts (1674-1748) that begins with "Lord, I am Thine, but Thou wilt prove."

Preface

Courteous Reader,

Although this is a small book, yet it presents you with matters of the greatest and most weighty concern, even with a discourse of life and death to eternity. It reveals and clarifies, by the Scriptures of God, that the time is at hand when there will be a resurrection of the dead, both of the just and unjust – even of the bodies of both, from the graves where they are, or will be, at the start of that day.

In these few lines, you also have the order and manner of the rising of these two types of people, wherein it is shown to you with great clearness with what body they will then rise, as well as their condition at that day.

You will here see the truth, including the manner of the terrible judgment, the opening of the books, and the examining of witnesses, with a final conclusion upon good and bad. I hope this will be profitable to the souls of those who read it. If you are godly, then through God's blessing, this will encourage you to go on in the faith of the truth of the gospel; but if you are ungodly, then you may meet with conviction, and you will see what will be, without fail, your end at the end of the world whether you continue in your sins or repent. If you continue in your sins, you will meet with despair, darkness, and everlasting destruction; but if you repent and believe the gospel, then you will find light, life, joy, comfort, glory, and happiness throughout all eternity.

Therefore, let me now urge upon you some admonitions:

First, that you take heed of that spirit of mockery that says, *Where is the promise of his coming?* (2 Peter 3:4).

Secondly, take heed that your heart is not *overcharged with surfeiting, and drunkenness, and cares of this life, and so that day come upon you unawares* (Luke 21:34-35).

Thirdly, be diligent in making *your calling and election sure* (2 Peter 1:10) so that in the day of which you will read more in this book, you will not be found without that glorious righteousness that will put you in good standing before God and will present you before His glorious presence with exceeding joy. To Him be glory in the church by Christ Jesus, world without end. Amen.

—John Bunyan

Of the Resurrection of the Dead

But this I confess unto thee, that after the way which
they call heresy, so worship I the God of my fathers,
believing all things which are written in the law and
in the prophets: and have hope toward God, which
they themselves also allow, that there shall be a res-
urrection of the dead, both of the just and unjust.
– Acts 24:14-15

My discussion upon this text will primarily concern the resurrection of the dead. I will immediately apply myself to that, not meddling with what else is expressed in the words.

You see here that Paul, being arraigned and accused of many things by some who were violent for his blood, and being permitted to speak for himself by the then heathen magistrate, tells them in a few words that he was entirely innocent concerning the crimes with which they charged him. He simply confessed that he worshipped the God of his fathers after that way that they call heresy, and that believing all things that are written in the Law and the Prophets, he had the same hope toward God that they themselves accepted – that there will be *a resurrection of the dead, both of the just and unjust.*

By the way, we can note from this that a hypocritical people will persecute the power of those truths in others that they themselves profess in words. I have hope toward God, and it is such a hope that they themselves allow, yet I am this day, and for this very thing, persecuted by them.

But to come to my purpose, *There shall be a resurrection of the dead.* By these words, the apostle shows us the substance of his doctrine – that there would be *a resurrection of the dead.* Also by these words concerning the doctrine of a resurrection, the apostle Paul shows what was the great argument with his soul that would carry him through these temptations, afflictions, reproaches, and necessities he met with in this world – the doctrine of a resurrection. He said that he had *hope toward God,* and there his mind was fixed, for *there shall be a resurrection of the dead, both of the just and unjust.* The reason why he could not do what these Jews wanted him to do, and also why he could not live as the gentiles do, is because he had the faith of the resurrection in his soul. This is the doctrine that made him fear to offend and that supported his soul, keeping him from destruction and confusion under all the storms and tempests he went through in this life. In a word, this had more impact upon his conscience than all the laws of men with all the penalties they inflict. *And herein do I exercise myself, to have always a conscience void of offence toward God and toward men* (Acts 24:16).

Now since we see that this doctrine of the resurrection of the dead has the power both to support us through this life and to impact our lives, to encourage the spirit and the body of the people of God, and to keep us on the right path, it will be necessary and profitable for us to inquire into the true meaning and nature of *the resurrection of the dead.*

To better understand this matter, I will briefly examine:

- What in this verse is meant by the *dead*.

- What is meant by the *resurrection*.

- Why the apostle Paul speaks here of the resurrection of the dead as of something yet to come: *There shall be a resurrection of the dead, both of the just and unjust.*

First: The ***dead*** in Scripture go under a fivefold consideration:

1. There are those who die a natural death, or as when someone ceases to be in this world any longer, as David, whom Peter tells us *is both dead and buried, and his sepulchre is with us to this day* (Acts 2:29).

2. There is a people who are considered dead in trespasses and sins, as those who have not yet been transformed from darkness to light and from the power of Satan to God. They have never yet felt the power of the Word and Spirit of God to raise them from that condition, to walk with Him in regeneration, making a life out of Christ and His present benefits (Ephesians 2:1-2; John 5:25).

   > Mention is made in Scripture of a death to sin and the lusts of the flesh. This death is the beginning of true life and happiness.

3. There is a death that seizes people often after some measure of light has been received from God, and after some profession of the gospel of Christ. These, for the certainty of their damnation, are said to be dead – dead, *twice dead*, and *plucked up by the roots* (Jude 1:12).

4. Mention is made in Scripture of a death to sin and the lusts of the flesh. This death is the beginning of true

life and happiness and is a certain forerunner of a portion in Christ and being with Him in another world (Romans 6:6-8; 2 Timothy 2:11).

5. Lastly, there is also a relation of eternal death in the Word. This is the death that those are in, and are swallowed up by, who leave this world godless, Christless, and graceless. They die in sin, and so are under the curse of the dreadful God. Because they have ignored the Lord Jesus Christ, the Savior, in this day of grace, they are fallen into the gulf and jaws of eternal death and misery, in *the fire that never shall be quenched* (Mark 9:43-44; Luke 16:23-26).

Since death, or to be dead, is taken under so many considerations in the Scriptures, it is evident that all of the texts are not referring to being dead in Christ. I then must distinguish and inquire which of these deaths it is that the apostle Paul is looking for a resurrection from in our text.

a. It cannot mean a resurrection from eternal death, for from that there is no redemption (Psalm 49:8).

b. Neither is it a resurrection from that double death, for those who are in that are past recovery also.

c. As for those who are dead to sin, it is nonsense to say there will or can be a resurrection from that, for that itself is a resurrection, and Paul had then already passed through that resurrection. As he also said, God has made alive all the brethren, who were dead in trespasses and sins (Colossians 2:12-13, 20). He also wrote, *If ye then be risen with Christ* (Colossians 3:1), and *Wherein also ye are risen with him, through the faith of the operation of God, who hath raised him from the dead* (Colossians 2:12).

d. Therefore, the dead in this verse must be understood as those who have departed this life, whose body and soul have separated from each other. The resurrection, then, must be a resurrection of the body out of the grave. As Daniel says, *Many of them that sleep in the dust of the earth shall awake* (Daniel 12:2). Also, *The hour is coming, in the which all that are in the graves shall hear his voice, and shall come forth, they that have done good, unto the resurrection of life; and they that have done evil, unto the resurrection of damnation* (John 5:28-29).

Second: What is meant by the **resurrection**?

The resurrection of the just is the rising of the bodies of the just; the resurrection of the unjust is the rising of their bodies at the last judgment. This also is the meaning of that saying of Paul to Agrippa: *I stand and am judged for the hope of the promise made of God unto our fathers* (Acts 26:6). That promise first began to be fulfilled in the resurrection of the body of Christ (Acts 13:32-33), and has its fulfillment when the dead, small and great, are raised out of their graves. Wherefore, although Paul says in Acts 13 that it is already ful-filled, here he says that he hopes it will come: *Which promise our twelve tribes, instantly serving God day and night, hope to come* (Acts 26:7). As God told Daniel, *Go thy way till the end be: for thou shalt rest and stand in thy lot at the end of the days* (Daniel 12:13).

> Christ is risen, therefore the promise is fulfilled that far, but His saints are still in their graves, and therefore that part of its fulfilling is still to come.

Christ is already risen, and therefore the promise is fulfilled that far, but His saints are still in their graves, and therefore that part of its fulfilling is still to come. As Paul said, *Why should it be thought a thing incredible with you, that God should raise the dead?* (Acts 26:8).

It is further evident that this verse refers to the resurrection of the dead bodies of both saints and sinners because the apostle says that it is the resurrection that the very Pharisees themselves acknowledged. Paul said, I *have hope toward God, which themselves also allow.* Then in his next words, he shows what that hope is – *that there shall be a resurrection of the dead, both of the just and unjust.*

We know that the Pharisees did not acknowledge a resurrection from a state of nature to a state of grace, which is the same with the new birth, but they did confidently acknowledge and teach that they were the children of Abraham according to the flesh. When any of them began to maintain or hold to Christ's doctrine in some things, they would still be troubled by the doctrine of the new birth or of being raised from a state of nature to a state of grace. In the meantime, though, they were utterly against the doctrine of the Sadducees that denied the resurrection of the body (John 3:1-9; John 8:51-56; Acts 23:6-8).

Further, the resurrection spoken of here must necessarily be the resurrection of the body because it is called *a resurrection of the dead, both of the just and unjust* – that is, of both saints and sinners. This is in accord with the words of Christ when He said, *The hour is coming, in the which all that are in the graves shall hear his voice, and shall come forth; they that have done good, unto the resurrection of life; and they that have done evil, unto the resurrection of damnation* (John 5:28-29).

Third: The resurrection spoken of is something yet to come.

The resurrection mentioned here is a resurrection to come; it is not already experienced, either by saints or sinners: *There shall be a resurrection of the dead, both of the just and unjust.* The resurrection here being still waited for by the just, yet also called *the resurrection of the dead, both of the just and unjust,* must necessarily be the same resurrection that is spoken of by Job, who said, *So man lieth down, and riseth not: till the heavens be no more, they shall not awake, nor be raised out of their sleep* (Job 14:12).

Having briefly opened this passage of Scripture unto you, and for the further satisfaction of those who are still wavering, as well as for the refreshment of those who are strong and steadfast, I will next provide you with several undeniable Scripture demonstrations of the resurrection of the dead, both of the just and the unjust.

The Resurrection of the Just

First, the just must arise because Christ is risen from the dead. Christ is the head of the just, and they are the members of His body. Therefore, because of this union, the just must arise. This is the apostle's own argument. He says, *If Christ be preached that he rose from the dead, how say some among you that there is no resurrection of the dead? But if there be no resurrection of the dead, then is Christ not risen* (1 Corinthians 15:12-13).

The reason why the apostle argues for the resurrection from the dead because of the resurrection of Christ is because the saints, of whose resurrection he here mainly speaks, are the members of Christ in their bodies, as well as in their souls. Paul writes, *Know ye not that your bodies are the members of Christ?* (1 Corinthians 6:15). This is a very significant argument, for if a good man is a member of Christ, then he must either be raised out of his grave, or else sin and death must have power over the members of Christ.

If this body is not raised, then Christ is not a complete conqueror over His enemies, for then death and the grave still have power over His members. *The last enemy that shall be destroyed is death* (1 Corinthians 15:26). Although Christ in His own person has a complete conquest over death, death still has power over the bodies of all who are in their graves. If Christ is considered in relation to His members, then He does not yet have a complete conquest over death, and He will not until everyone is brought forth out of their graves; for then, and not until then, will that saying be fulfilled in every way that *death is swallowed up in victory* (1 Corinthians 15:54).

Second, there must be a resurrection of the just because the bodies of the saints, as well as their souls, are the purchase of Christ's blood.

Ye are bought with a price: therefore glorify God in your body, and in your spirit, which are God's (1 Corinthians 6:20). Christ will not lose that which He purchased with His blood. "O death," Christ says, "I will have them. O grave, I will make you let them go. I will ransom them from the power of the grave. I will redeem them from death. I have bought them, and they will be Mine."

O death, I will be thy plagues; O grave, I will be thy destruction (Hosea 13:14). Even if the power of the grave would be invincible, and if death would be *the king of terrors* (Job 18:14), yet the *issues from death* belong to Him who has *the keys of hell and of death* (Revelation 1:18). *He that is our God is the God of salvation; and unto GOD the Lord belong the issues from death* (Psalm 68:20) – and we, the price of His blood, will be delivered.

Third, the body is the temple of the Holy Spirit, which is in us.

What? Know ye not that your body is the temple of the Holy Ghost which is in you, which ye have of God, and ye are not your own? (1 Corinthians 6:19). The body is not such a ridiculous thing in Christ's estimation as it was in the estimation of the Sadducees. *The body is not for fornication, but for the Lord; and the Lord for the body* (1 Corinthians 6:13). This is true not only in this world, but also in the world that is to come. That is why Paul said, *God hath both raised up the Lord, and will also raise us up by his own power* (1 Corinthians 6:14); that is, as He has raised up the body of Christ, so He will also raise up ours by Christ.

Fourth, the bodies of the just must arise again because of that likeness that is between the body of the Lord Jesus Christ and the bodies of the saints.

When he shall appear, we shall be like him (1 John 3:2). It is abundantly clear in Scripture that the body of the Lord Jesus was raised out of the grave, caught up into heaven, and always remains a glorified body in the holiest of all (Luke 24:3-7, 36-43; John 20:24-28; Acts 1:2-11; 2:31; 17:30-32; Mark 16:6-7, 19; Hebrews 7:24-26; 8:1-3; 10:12).

It would be very strange to me if Christ would be raised, ascended, and glorified in that body, yet that His people would be with Him only in their spirits – especially since He in His resurrection is said to be but *the firstborn from the dead* (Colossians 1:18) and the firstfruits of those who sleep (1 Corinthians 15:20, 23). We know that a *first* begotten implies more children, and that *first*fruits indicates a later crop. Therefore we conclude that *as in Adam all die, even so in Christ shall all be made alive. But every man in his own order: Christ the firstfruits; afterward they that are Christ's at his coming* (1 Corinthians 15:22-23).

This is why the Scripture says that He *shall change our vile body, that it may be fashioned like unto his glorious body* (Philippians 3:21), and why the day of Christ is said to be the day of the *manifestation of the sons of God* (Romans 8:19) and of *the redemption of our body* (Romans 8:23). Then the saints of God will not only be as their Savior, but will also appear as their Savior, being delivered from their graves, as He is from His, and glorified in their bodies, as He is in His.

Fifth, there must be a resurrection of the body of the saints because the body, as well as the mind, has shared deeply in the afflictions that we meet with for the gospel's sake.

Yes, and the body often suffers more in all the afflictions that we experience for Christ's sake here. It is the body that feels the prison chains, the whip, the torture, hunger and cold, and a thousand other afflictions. It is in the body that we have the dying *marks of the Lord Jesus* (Galatians 6:17), *that the life also of Jesus might be made manifest in our mortal flesh* (2 Corinthians 4:11). God is such a just God, and is so merciful to His people, that even though the bodies of His saints would, through the enmity of the enemy, be dishonorably tortured, killed, and sown in the grave, yet He will, as will be soon shown, raise it again in incorruption, glory, and honor.

> God is such a just God, that even though the bodies of His saints would be dishonorably tortured and killed, yet He will raise it again in glory and honor.

As He says also in another place, we who have continued with Christ in His temptations, who have for His sake undergone the reproach and enmity of the world, to you, Christ says, *I appoint unto you a kingdom, as my Father hath appointed unto me* (Luke 22:28-29). *If we suffer, we shall also reign with him* (2 Timothy 2:12), and *he that hateth his life in this world shall keep it unto life eternal* (John 12:25). All this is to be enjoyed, especially at the resurrection of the just.

Sixth, there must be a resurrection of the just; otherwise, there will be the greatest disappointment on all sides that ever was since man has been on the earth.

1. It would be a disappointment of the will of God. Jesus said, *And this is the Father's will which hath sent me, that of all* *which he hath given me I should lose nothing* [not even a speck of dust], *but should raise it up again at the last day* (John 6:39).

2. It would be a disappointment of the power of God. He who has raised up the Lord Jesus also intends to raise us up, even our bodies, by His power. As Paul says, *The body is not for fornication, but for the Lord; and the Lord for the body. And God hath both raised up the Lord, and will also raise up us by his own power* (1 Corinthians 6:13-14).

3. If there would be no resurrection of the just, Christ also would be extremely disappointed of the fruits of all His sufferings. As I told you before, His people are the price of His blood and the members of His body, and He is now at the right hand of God, *far above all principality, and power, and might, and dominion, and every name that is named* (Ephesians 1:21), watching and waiting until His enemies are made

> How disappointed Jesus would be if, when He comes, the grave would keep down those whom He has ransomed with His blood!

His footstool (Hebrews 1:13) and are brought under the foot of the weakest saint, which will not be until the last enemy, death, is destroyed.

We know that when He went away He said that He would come again and bring all His people to Himself, even up into heaven, that where He is, there we may be also (John 12:26; 14:1-3; 17:24). How disappointed He would be if, when He comes, the grave and death would prevent and hinder Him, and with its bars, keep down those whom He has ransomed with His blood from the power of His blood!

4. If the bodies of the just do not arise from the dead, then they also will be disappointed. It is true that the departed saints have far more fellowship and communion with God and the Lord Jesus than we have, or are not yet capable of having, since they are in paradise and we in this world (Luke 23:43), yet for all that, although they are there, they are very much longing for the day of the Lord's vengeance, which will be the day in which they will, and must, arise from the dead.

This is the time that they long for, when they cry under the altar, *How long, O Lord, holy and true, dost thou not judge and avenge our blood on them that dwell on the earth?* (Revelation 6:10). When they died, they died in hope to *obtain a better resurrection* (Hebrews 11:35), and now that they are gone, they long for that day when the dead, even all the enemies of Christ, will be judged; for then He will give rewards to His servants the prophets, and to His saints, and to all who fear His name, both small and great (Revelation 11:18).

5. If the just do not arise, great disappointment also will be to the saints still alive in this world. The reason for this is because even though they have already received the firstfruits of the Spirit, yet they wait not only for more of that, but also for the resurrection, redemption, and changing of this vile body. Paul wrote, *For our conversation is in heaven; from whence also we look for the Savior, the Lord Jesus Christ: who shall change our vile body, that it may be fashioned like unto his glorious body* (Philippians 3:20-21).

If the body does not rise, then how can it be made like the glorious body of Christ Jesus? Yes, what a sad disappointment, desire, and delusion those poor creatures are under who look for such a thing, and do so based upon the Word of God! They look for good, but behold evil (Job 30:26). They expect to be delivered in their whole person from every enemy, but behold – both death and the grave, their great enemies, swallow them up for ever.

Beloved, do not be deceived. *The needy shall not always be forgotten: the expectation of the poor shall not perish for ever* (Psalm 9:18). Christ says that he who *seeth the Son, and believeth on him that sent him, may have everlasting life: and I will raise him up at the last day* (John 6:40).

6. If the just do not arise out of their graves, then every grace of God in our souls is defeated. For although the spirit of devotion can put forth a pretended show of holiness with the denial of the resurrection, yet every grace of God in the elect spurs them forward to live as is fitting of the gospel by pointing at this day.

1. It is this that faith looks at, according as it is written, *I believed, and therefore have I spoken; we also believe, and therefore speak; knowing that he which raised up the Lord Jesus shall raise up us also by Jesus, and shall present us with you* (2 Corinthians 4:13-14).

2. Hope looks at this. Paul wrote, *[We] which have the firstfruits of the Spirit, even we ourselves groan within ourselves, waiting for the adoption, to wit, the redemption of our body [that is, we expect this by hope]. For we are saved by hope: but hope that is seen is not hope: for what a man seeth [or has in present possession], why doth he yet hope for?* (Romans 8:23-24).

3. The grace of self-denial also works by this doctrine. *If after the manner of men I have fought with beasts at Ephesus, what advantageth it me, if the dead rise not?* (1 Corinthians 15:32). This is as if to say, "Why do I deny myself of those mercies and privileges that the people of this world enjoy? Why do not I also avoid persecution for the cross of Christ like they do? If the dead do not

rise, how will I be any better off for all my trouble that I meet with here for the gospel of Christ?

4. Both zeal and patience, along with all other the graces of the Spirit of God in our hearts, are generally much encouraged, awakened, and supported by this doctrine. As James says, *Be patient, therefore, brethren, unto the coming of the Lord* (James 5:7), for it is then that the dead will be raised (1 Thessalonians 4:16-17). *Behold, the husbandman waiteth for the precious fruit of the earth, and hath long patience for it, until he receive the early and latter rain. Be ye also patient; stablish your hearts; for the coming of the Lord draweth nigh* (James 5:7-8).

7. The doctrine of the resurrection of the just must necessarily be a certain truth of God if we consider the wicked and satanical errors and absurdities that must unavoidably follow the denial thereof, such as he who does not believe in the resurrection of our bodies denies the resurrection of the body of Christ.

This is the Spirit's own doctrine: *For if the dead rise not, then is not Christ raised* (1 Corinthians 15:16). He who denies the resurrection of the members of the body denies the resurrection of the head, for since the resurrection of the saints is proved by the resurrection of Christ, he who denies the resurrection of the saints must necessarily deny the resurrection of Christ that proves it. Now this error, which is in itself destructive to all Christian religion, is like an adder, for it carries within its bowels many other errors that are similarly wicked and indecent. Some of these awful errors are described below:

> He who denies the resurrection of the saints must necessarily deny the resurrection of Christ that proves it.

1. He who denies the resurrection of the saints concludes that to preach deliverance from sin and death is useless preaching, for how can someone be freed from sin if he is swallowed up forever by death and the grave? He most certainly is always confined in death and the grave if Christ is not risen, for His resurrection is the basis of ours. As Paul says, *If Christ be not risen, then is our preaching vain, and your faith is also vain* (1 Corinthians 15:14). If Christ is not risen, then we preach fables and you receive them as truth.

2. This error casts the lie in the face of God, of Christ, and the Scriptures. *Yea, and we are found false witnesses of God; because we have testified of God that he raised up Christ: whom he raised not up, if so be that the dead rise not* (1 Corinthians 15:15). Notice that earlier Paul said that Christ in His resurrection proves our resurrection, but now he says that our resurrection will prove the truth of His. Indeed, both are true – for as by Christ's rising, ours is affirmed, and by ours, His is demonstrated.

3. The denial of the resurrection also condemns to eternal destruction all those who have departed this world in the faith of this doctrine. *If Christ be not raised [as if He is not, we rise not, then not only] your faith is vain; ye are yet in your sins [those who are alive]. Then they also which are fallen asleep in Christ are perished* (1 Corinthians 15:17-18).

4. He who denies the resurrection of the just concludes that the Christian is of all people the most miserable. *If in this life only we have hope in Christ, we are of all men most miserable* (1 Corinthians 15:19). First of all, *if the dead rise not*, we would be the most miserable because we let go of present enjoyments for those that will never come. We would be the most miserable people *if the dead rise*

not because our faith, our hope, our joy, and our peace would all be a lie.

But you will say that he who gives himself up to God will have comfort in this life. Ah, but *if the dead rise not*, all our comfort that we now think we have from God will then be found to be presumption and foolishness because we believe that God has so loved us as to have us in His day, in body and soul, to heaven – and this will not be so *if the dead rise not.*

If in this life only we have hope in Christ, we are of all men most miserable. Poor Christian! You who look for the *blessed hope* of the resurrection of the body, *and the glorious appearing of the great God and our Savior Jesus Christ* (Titus 2:13), how you will be deceived *if the dead rise not! But now is Christ risen from the dead, and become the firstfruits of them that slept. For since by man came death, by man came also the resurrection of the dead* (1 Corinthians 15:20-21).

5. He who denies the resurrection of the dead opens a floodgate to all manner of impiety. He cuts the throat of a truly holy life and lays the reins upon the neck of the most shameful lusts, for if the dead rise not, let us eat and drink. That is, let us do anything, no matter how evil and vile: *let us eat and drink; for tomorrow we die* (1 Corinthians 15:32), and that will be the end of us. We will not arise again to receive either evil or good.

6. To deny this resurrection, if someone simply says it is already past, either with him or any Christian, his saying so contributes directly to the destruction and overthrow of the faith of those who hear him, and it is so far from being according to the doctrine of God, that it destroys good and wholesome doctrine just as disease can eat the

face and flesh of a man. How unsightly they look who have their nose and lips eaten off with disease! Even so badly does the doctrine of no resurrection of the dead look in the eyes of God, Christ, saints, and Scripture (2 Timothy 2:18).

7. I conclude then, that to deny the resurrection of the bodies of the just asserts the following:

Denying the resurrection demonstrates great ignorance of God. It shows ignorance of His power to raise, ignorance of His promise to raise, and ignorance of His faithfulness to raise – and that in regard to Himself, His Son, and the saints, as I showed before. That is why Paul wrote to those who were deluded in this way, *Awake to righteousness, and sin not; for some have not the knowledge of God. I speak this to your shame* (1 Corinthians 15:34).

It is as if he had said, "Do you profess Christianity, and do you question the resurrection of the body? Do you not know that the resurrection of the body, and the glory to follow, is the very essence of the gospel of Jesus Christ? Are you ignorant of the resurrection of the Lord Jesus, and do you question the power and faithfulness of God, both to His Son and His saints, because you say there will be no resurrection of the dead? You are ignorant of God – of what He can do, of what He will do, and of how He will glorify Himself by doing so.

> Just as denying the resurrection demonstrates very great ignorance of God's power, so it demonstrates blatant ignorance of the heart of the Scriptures.

Just as denying the resurrection demonstrates very great ignorance of God's power, faithfulness, etc., so it demonstrates blatant ignorance of the heart and direction of the Scriptures. As Jesus explained, *As touching the dead, that they rise: have ye not read in the book of Moses how in the bush God spake unto him, saying, I am the God of Abraham, and the God of Isaac, and the God of Jacob? He is not the God of the dead, but the God of the living: ye therefore do greatly err* (Mark 12:26-27).

It is to be understood that being the God of Abraham, Isaac, and Jacob means to be their God under a new covenant consideration. As He says, *I will be their God, and they shall be my people* (2 Corinthians 2:16). He is not the God of the dead – that is, of those who perish – whether they are angels or men (Hosea 6:2; John 8:42; Colossians 3:4; Hebrews 8:10-11).

Those who are the children of God, as Abraham, Isaac, and Jacob, are called the living under a threefold consideration:

a. They are called the living in their Lord and head, and so all the elect may be said to live; for they are chosen in Him from eternity, who also is their life, though possibly many of them are still unconverted. Christ is their life by the eternal purpose of God.

b. The children of the new covenant live both in their spirits in glory by open vision, and here by faith and the continual communication of grace from Christ into their souls (Galatians 2:20).

c. They live also with respect to their rising again, for God *calleth those things which be not as though they were* (Romans 4:17). To be born, dead, buried, risen, and ascended are all in the present with God. He does not live by time, as we do; a thousand years to Him are but as the day that is past. *One day is with the Lord as a thousand years* (2 Peter 3:8). Eternity, which is God Himself, acknowledges no first, second, and third; all things are naked and bare before Him (Hebrews 4:13) and present with Him (Isaiah 46:9-10). All who are His live unto Him. *There shall be a resurrection of the dead, both of the just and unjust* (Acts 24:15).

A resurrection of what? Is it a resurrection of that which is sown, or of that which was never sown? If it is of that which is sown, then it must be either of that nature that was sown, or else of the corruption that clings to it; but if it is the nature, and not the corruption that clings to it, then that rises again. Truly, the very term "resurrection" is a powerful argument to prove that the dead will come forth out of their graves, for the Holy Spirit has always spoken more properly than to say, *There shall be a resurrection of the dead, both of the just and unjust,* if neither the good nor the bad will come forth out of their graves, but rather means something else to mislead the world.

The Manner of the Resurrection of the Just

T he apostle Paul, after he had proven the truth and certainty of the resurrection in 1 Corinthians 15, went on to explain the manner of it. In order to remove those foolish doubts that accompany the hearts of the ignorant, he begins with one of their questions: *But some man will say, How are the dead raised up? and with what body do they come?* (1 Corinthians 15:35).

Paul answered this first by comparing it to a seed that is sown in the earth. In this comparison, he mentioned three things:

1. That our reviving or rising must be after death: *That which thou sowest is not quickened except it die* (v. 36).

2. That at our rising, we will not only revive and live, but we will be changed into a far more glorious state than when we were sown: *That which thou sowest, thou sowest not that body that shall be, . . . but God giveth it a body as it hath pleased him* (vv. 37-38). That is, He gives the body more splendor, radiance, and beauty at its resurrection.

3. However, neither its enlivening nor its transcendent splendor will hinder it from being the same body, as to

its nature, that was sown in the earth; for as God gives it a body for honor and splendor as it pleases Him, so He gives *to every seed his own body* (v. 38).

Indeed, this analogy by which he here affirms the manner of the resurrection of the just is very natural, and is appropriate in each detail. As to its burial, (1) The corn of wheat is first dead, and afterward is sown and buried in the earth. So is the body of man. (2) After the corn is dead and buried, then it is vitalized and revived to life. So also it will be with our bodies, for after the body is laid in the grave and buried, it will then be vitalized and will rise and revive.

As to the manner of its change in its rising, this comparison is also very appropriate. It is sown a dead kernel of wheat; it is raised a living one. It is sown dry and without beauty; it rises green and beautiful. It is sown a single kernel; it rises a full ear. It is sown in its covering; but in rising, it leaves that shell behind.

Further, although the kernel dies, is buried, and meets with all this change and alteration in these things, yet none of these changes can cause the nature of the kernel to cease; it remains wheat. Wheat was sown, and wheat arises. The difference is that it was sown dead, dry, and barren wheat, but it rises living, beautiful, and fruitful wheat. It has this alteration, then, that it greatly changes its resemblance, although it still has this power to retain its own nature. God gives it a body as it pleases Him, *and to every seed his own body.*

The apostle in this way presented the manner of the resurrection of the saints by the nature of seed sown and rising again.

Second, to explain further, Paul gave three more analogies.

The first is to show us the variety and glory of fleshly appearance. The second is to show us the difference of glory that is between heavenly bodies and those that are of the earth. The third is to show us the difference that is between the glory of the light of the sun from that of the moon, and also how one star differs from another in glory, concluding with *so is the resurrection of the dead* (1 Corinthians 15:42). This is to say that at the resurrection of the bodies, the bodies will be altered and changed more abundantly than if the flesh of beasts and fowls were made as noble as the flesh of men; or if the bodies of earth were made as excellent as the heavenly bodies; or if the glory of the moon would be made as bright and as clear as the glory of the sun; or as if the glory of the feeblest star was as glorious and as shining as the biggest in the firmament of heaven.

It is a resurrection indeed – a resurrection in every way. As to its nature, the body arises to the self-same nature; but as to its manner – how far superior it is! A poor, dry, wrinkled kernel is cast into the ground, and there it lies and swells and breaks and, one would think, perishes; but behold, it receives life! It sprouts, puts forth a blade, and grows into a stalk. Then there appears an ear. It also sweetly blossoms with a full kernel in the ear.

It is the same wheat, yet behold how the form and fashion of that which now arises differs from that which was then sown. Its glory also when it was sown is no glory when compared with that in which it rises. Yet it is the same that rises that was sown, and no other, although it is the same after a far more glorious manner. It is not the same with its husk, but without it. Our bran will be left behind us when we rise again.

Wherefore, at our rising, we will not change our nature, but our glory.

The comparison also between the heavenly and earthly bodies teaches the same. *The glory of the celestial is one, and the glory of the terrestrial is another* (1 Corinthians 15:40). Now notice that Paul does not speak here of the natures of each of these bodies, but of the transcendent glory of one above another. *The glory of the celestial [heavenly] is one, and the glory of the*

25

terrestrial [earthly] is another. Wherefore, at our rising, we will not change our nature, but our glory. We will be equal to the angels (Luke 20:36), not with respect to their nature, but their glory. The nature also of the moon is one thing, and the glory of the moon is another; and so *one star differeth from another in glory* (1 Corinthians 15:41).

A beggar has the same nature as a king, and gold in the ore has the same nature as that which is best refined; but the beggar does not have the same glory with the king, nor does the gold in ore have the same glory with that which is refined. However, our state will be far more altered than any of these in the days when we, like so many suns in the firmament of heaven, arise out of the heart and bowels of the earth.

If you consider these things, you see how futilely they argue who say that our human nature, consisting of body and soul, will not inherit the kingdom of God. You can also see how far from their purpose that saying of the apostle Paul is, that *flesh and blood cannot inherit the kingdom of God* (1 Corinthians 15:50). Now because I have mentioned the objection itself, I will not pass by it without discussing it briefly.

Therefore, reader, whoever you are, consider that frequently in Scripture the words "flesh" and "blood," as also in the verse recently mentioned, are not to be understood of that matter that God made – the flesh that clings to our bones and the blood that runs in our veins. Rather, it refers to that corruption, weakness, mortality, and evil that clings to it. This weakness and corruption possesses all people, and also completely rules where the soul is unconverted; therefore it bears the name of that which is ruled and acted by it – that is, our whole man, consisting of body and soul.

This is something distinct from that flesh and blood that is essential to our being, and without which we are not human. For example, Paul says that he who is Christ's has *crucified the flesh with the affections and lusts* (Galatians 5:24). Who is so vain as to think that the apostle Paul by these words was referring to our material flesh that hangs on our bones and is mixed with our natural blood, sinews, and veins – and not rather of that inward fountain of sin, corruption, and wickedness that in another place he calls *the old man* with his *deceitful lusts* (Ephesians 4:22)? Paul also said, *The flesh lusteth against the Spirit, and the Spirit against the flesh* (Galatians 5:17).

Is it our flesh that hangs on our bones that lusts (strives) against the Spirit? Is it that flesh that the Spirit strives against? Certainly, if the Spirit strives against our material flesh, then it is our duty not to nourish it at all, because by nourishing it, we nourish that against which the Spirit of God fights and wars. If the Spirit strives against the flesh on our bones that is simply considered as flesh, and if it is our duty to follow the Spirit, then we must necessarily kill ourselves or cut our flesh from our bones. For whatever the Spirit of God strives against must be destroyed. Yes, it is our duty to quickly destroy it.

But know, O vain man, that by flesh here is to be understood not the nature that God has made, but the corrupt apprehension and wisdom, along with those inclinations to evil, that lodge within us, which are also called the wisdom of the flesh. Yes, in plain terms, they are called *flesh and blood*, where Christ says, *Flesh and blood hath not revealed [this] unto thee, but my Father which is in heaven* (Matthew 16:17).

Observe that all these places, and many others, point to a corrupt soul rather than a corrupt body. Indeed, sin and all spiritual wickedness have their seat in the heart and soul of a person, and by their using this or that member of the body, so defile the person. The weaknesses of the body, or those that attend our material flesh and blood, are weaknesses of another kind, such as sickness, aches, pains, sores, wounds, etc. Therefore, where you read of flesh and blood as rejected by God, especially when it speaks of the flesh and blood of saints, you are not to understand it as meaning the flesh, which is their proper human nature, but of that weakness that clings to it.

In another place, Paul lists the works of the flesh in many things, such as in witchcraft, hatred, variance, strife, jealousy, fornication, and many others (Galatians 5:19-20). But can anyone imagine that in that passage of Scripture Paul would be opposing the flesh that hangs on our bones? No. Rather, he is speaking of that sin and rebellion that is in the mind of man against the Lord, by reason of which the members of the body are used to accomplish its most filthy and offensive deeds. They were *enemies in [their] mind by wicked works* (Colossians 1:21).

You can see that "flesh and blood" is not always to be taken for the flesh that is upon our hands, feet, and other parts of our body, but often refers to that sin, weakness, and infirmity that clings to our whole person.

Further then, regarding our real, substantial flesh, it may be either considered as God's creature purely, or as corrupted with sin and infirmity. If you consider it as corrupted, it will not inherit the kingdom of God; yet if you consider it as God's creature, then you know that all whom God has converted to Himself through Jesus Christ will, even with that body when changed, inherit the kingdom of God. The woman whose clothes are dirty can still distinguish between the dirt and the cloth on which the dirt rests – and this is how God deals with us.

It is true that there is not one saint whose body is not affected and infected with many corrupt and filthy things while he lives in this world in regard to bodily weaknesses. Yes, and all are also affected with many sinful weaknesses by reason of that body of sin and death that still remains in us. However, God still distinguishes between our weaknesses and His workmanship, and He knows how to save the whole man of His people while He is destroying the corruption and weakness that clings to them.

Let us now return to the place objected: *Flesh and blood shall not inherit the kingdom of God*. It cannot be truly understood that that flesh that is man's nature will not enter the kingdom, for then, as I said before, Christ must lose His members, the purchase of His blood, and the vessels and temples of His Spirit – for all this is our body. Again, then, this would mean that Christ also (in that His body, which is also our flesh and blood) is not in glory, contrary to the whole direction of the New Testament (Hebrews 2:14-15; 7:24-25; 8:3-4; 10:10-12; Revelation 1:18; 2:8).

Yes, it would be nonsense to say that there will be a resurrection and that our *vile body* will be changed and made *like unto* the *glorious body* of the Son of God if this body does not at all rise again, but something else rises, which is not in us, and our nature. But to get right to the point, when Paul here says, *Flesh and blood cannot inherit . . .* , he speaks properly of that mortality and weakness that now attends our whole man, and not of our real, substantial body itself. For after he had said, *Flesh and blood cannot inherit the kingdom of God*, he added, *neither doth corruption inherit incorruption*.

These two sayings are answerable to what he then adds, saying, *Behold, I shew you a mystery; we shall not all sleep, but we shall all be changed, in a moment, in the twinkling of an eye, at the last trump: for the trumpet shall sound, and the dead shall be raised incorruptible, and we shall be changed* (1 Corinthians 15:51-52). Notice that Paul says that it is the dead who will be raised incorruptible; that is, the dead will be so raised that in their rising, incorruption will possess them instead of corruption, and immortality instead of that mortality that descended to the grave with them – *for this corruptible must put on incorruption, and this mortal must put on immortality* (1 Corinthians 15:53).

Notice that Paul said *this corruptible*; it is *this corruptible, and this mortal*, that must be raised, though not raised corruptible and mortal as it was buried, but immortal and incorruptible. It will leave its graveclothes of corruption and mortality behind it.

Third, in describing the manner of their rising, the apostle Paul more distinctly branches out a little in four specific points:

1. It is sown in corruption; it is raised in incorruption.

2. It is sown in dishonor; it is raised in glory.

3. It is sown in weakness; it is raised in power.

4. It is sown a natural body; it is raised a spiritual body (1 Corinthians 15).

1. It is raised in incorruption. We are brought into this world by sin and corruption. Corruption is our father (Job 17:14), and in sin did our mother conceive us (Psalm 51:5). This is not only why our lives are like a span or shadow for shortness, but it is also why it is accompanied with so much *vanity and vexation of spirit* (Ecclesiastes 1:14). But now being raised from the dead incorruptible, which is also called a begetting and birth, these things that annoy us now in our life and eventually take away our life are effectually destroyed.

> These things that annoy us now in our life and eventually take away our life are effectually destroyed.

Therefore, we live forever, as the Spirit says, *and there shall be no more death, neither sorrow, nor crying, neither shall there be any more pain: for the former things,* that is, all our corruptibleness, *are passed away* (Revelation 21:4).

In our resurrection, there will not be any corruption either of body or of soul. There will be no weakness, nor sickness, nor anything like that. As the Bible says, Christ will present us *to himself a glorious church, not having spot, or wrinkle, or any such thing* (Ephesians 5:27). Therefore, when Paul says that the body is raised in incorruption, it is as if he had said that it is impossible that they should ever sin anymore, be sick anymore, sorrow anymore, or die anymore. *They which shall be counted worthy to obtain that world, and the resurrection from the dead, neither marry, nor are given in marriage*, although they could do so in this world; *neither can they die any more, for they are equal unto the angels; and are the children of God, being the children of the resurrection* (Luke 20:35-36).

2. It is raised in glory. The dishonor that accompanies the saint as he departs this world is very great: *he is sown in dishonour*. He is so abhorrent at his death that his dearest friends are weary of him, stop their noses at him, see no beauty in him, and set no price upon him (I speak nothing here how some of them are hanged, starved, banished, and so die, torn to pieces, and not permitted to be put into graves).

However, his body is raised in glory. Glory is the sweetness, beauty, purity, and perfection of a thing. The light is the glory of the sun, strength is the glory of youth, and grey hairs are the glory of old age (1 Corinthians 15:40-41; Proverbs 20:29). That is, it is the excellency of these things and is that which makes them shine.

Therefore, to arise in glory is first to arise in all the beauty and utmost completeness that is possible to possess a human creature. In all its features and parts, it is inconceivably beautiful. Sin and corruption have made zealous work in our bodies as well as in our souls. Sin is commonly the cause of all the flaws and ill-favoredness that now cling to us and that also renders us so dishonorable at our death. Now at our rising, though, being raised incorruptible, we will appear in such perfections, and that of all kinds, belonging to the body, that all the beauty and loveliness, sweetness and amiableness, that has been in this world at any time will be swallowed up a thousand times told with this glory.

The psalmist said of Christ that He was *fairer than the children of men* (Psalm 45:2). I believe that he was referring to His outward man as well as His inward part. He was the purest, most exact, most complete, and most beautiful creature that God ever made – until *his visage was so marred* by his persecutions (Isaiah 52:14), for in all things He had and will have the preeminence (Colossians 1:18). Our bodies at our resurrection will not only be as free from sin as His was before He died, but they will also be as free from all other infirmities as He was after He was raised again. In a word, if incorruptibleness can put a beauty upon our bodies when they arise, we will have it. There will be no lame legs, no sore shoulders, no cloudy eyes, and not even wrinkled faces. He *shall change our vile body, that it may be fashioned like unto his glorious body* (Philippians 3:21).

All the glory that a glorified soul can help this body to will be enjoyed at this day. That soul that has been in the heavens for hundreds or thousands of years, immersed in the presence of Christ, will in a moment come radiating into the body again and will inhabit every part and vein of the body as it did before its departure. The Spirit of God that also left the body when it went to the grave will now in all perfection dwell in this body again. I tell you that the body at this day will shine brighter than the face of Moses or Stephen (Exodus 34:29, 35; Acts 6:15) – even as bright as the sun, the stars, and the angels. *When Christ who is our life, shall appear, then shall ye also appear with him in glory* (Colossians 3:4; see also Daniel 12:3; Matthew 13:43; Luke 20:36).

3. It is raised in power. While we are here, we are accompanied with so many weaknesses and infirmities that in time, the littlest sin or sickness is too hard for us and takes away our strength, our beauty, our days, our breath, our life, and our all (Job 38:17). But behold, we are raised in power – in that power that all these things are as far below us as a grasshopper is below a giant (Numbers 13:33). At the first appearance of us, the world will tremble.

Behold, the gates of death and the bars of the grave are now carried away on our shoulders, just as Samson carried away the gates of the city (Judges 16:3). Death quakes and destruction falls down dead at our feet. What, then, can stand before us? We will then carry that grace, majesty, terror, and commanding power in our souls so that our countenances will be like lightning (Compare Luke 20:16 with Matthew 28:2-3). *For this corruptible must put on incorruption, and this mortal must put on immortality. So when this corruptible shall have put on incorruption, and this mortal shall have put on immortality, then shall be brought to pass the saying that is written, Death is swallowed up in victory* (1 Corinthians 15:53-54).

4. It is raised a spiritual body. This is the last point, and it is indeed the reason for the other three. It is an incorruptible body because it is a spiritual one. It is a glorious body because it is a spiritual one. It rises in power because it is a spiritual body. When the body is buried, or sown in the earth, it is a corruptible, dishonorable, weak, and natural body; but when it arises, it rises incorruptible, glorious, powerful, and spiritual.

As much as incorruption is above corruption, glory is above dishonor, power is above weakness, and spiritual is above natural, so great an alteration will there be in our body when raised again. Yet it is this body, and not another. It is this in nature, although changed into a far more glorious state, a thousand times further than if a keeper of swine were changed to be an emperor. Notice that *it is sown a natural body*. That is a very appropriate word, for although there dwells ever so much of the Spirit and grace of God in it while it lives, yet as soon as the soul is separate from it, so soon also does the Spirit of God separate from it, and will continue to be separated while the day of its rising is to come.

Therefore, it is laid into the earth a mere lump of man's nature – *It is sown a natural body* – but now at the day when *the heavens be no more* (Job 14:12), then the trump shall sound, even the trump of God, and in a moment, *the dead shall be raised incorruptible*, glorious, and spiritual (1 Corinthians 15:52; 1 Thessalonians 4:16-17). When the body arises, it will be so swallowed up by life and immortality that it will be as if it had lost its own human nature; although in truth, the same substantial real nature is every bit there still.

> The thing sweetened still retains its own proper nature, although by it being sweetened, it loses its former bitterness. That is how it will be with our bodies at the last day.

It is the same "it" that rises that was sown: *It is sown . . . , it is raised; it is sown . . . , it is raised*, says the apostle.

You know that things that are sweetened by the skill of the pharmacist are so immersed in the sweetness and virtue of that in which they are sweetened that they become as though they had no other nature than that in which they are boiled; the truth is, though, that the thing sweetened still retains its own proper nature and essence, although by virtue of its being sweetened, it loses its former sourness, bitterness, smell, or the like. In the same way, that is how it will be with our bodies at the last day. We will be so sweetened by being swallowed up by life, as we showed before, that we will be as if we were all spirit, when the truth is that this body will be swallowed up by life. It is necessary for our nature still to remain; otherwise, it cannot be us who will be in heaven, but will be something besides us. If we lose our proper human nature, then we absolutely lose our being, and so are annihilated into nothing. Wherefore it, the same "it" that is sown a natural body, will rise a spiritual body.

But again, as I said concerning things that are sweetened, our body, when thus risen, will lose all that sourness and vileness that now, by reason of sin and infirmity, clings to it. Neither will its unsteadiness or burdensomeness be any impediment to its acting after the manner of angels. Christ has shown us what our body at our resurrection will be, by showing us, in His Word, what His body was at and after His resurrection. We read that His body, after He was risen from the dead, although it still retained the very same flesh and bones that hung upon the cross, yet how angelic it was at all times and upon all occasions! He could enter in to where His disciples were with that very body when the doors were shut upon them. He could, at His pleasure and to their amazement, appear in the twinkling of an eye in the midst of them. He could be visible and invisible as He pleased when He sat to eat with them. In a word, He could pass and repass and ascend and descend in that body with far more pleasure and ease than the bird by the skill of her wing (Luke 24:31-32, 36-42, 50-51; John 20:19, 24-26; Acts 1:1-12; Mark 16:19; Ephesians 4:7-10).

Just as we have borne the image of our earthly father in this world, so, at that day, we will have the image of Jesus Christ and will be as He is: *As is the earthy, such are they also that are earthy: and as is the heavenly, such are they also that are heavenly. And as we have borne the image of the earthy, we shall also [at our resurrection] bear the image of the heavenly* (1 Corinthians 15:48-49). It is so in part now, but will so be in perfection then.

To ascend up to heaven, and to descend again when we desire, will be common with us in that day. If there were ten thousand bars of iron, or walls of brass, separating us from our pleasure and desire at that day, they would as easily be penetrated by us as is the cobweb, or the air by the beams of the sun. The reason for this is because to the Spirit, with whom we will be inconceivably filled at that day, nothing is impossible (Matthew 17:20).

In that day, it will be carried out in that nature and measure as to swallow up all impossibilities. He *shall change our vile body, that it may be fashioned like unto his glorious body,* [now notice this:] *according to the working whereby he is able even to subdue all things unto himself* (Philippians 3:21). It is as if we would say, "I know that there are many things that hinder us in this world from having our bodies like the body of Christ, but when God will raise us from the dead, because He will then have our bodies like the body of His Son, He will stretch forth such a power to work upon, and in, our bodies that He will remove all impossibilities and hindrances."

Even more, we do not only see what work the Spirit will have in our body by the actions of Christ after His resurrection, but even by many saints before their death. The Spirit used to carry Elijah away, no man could tell where he would go (1 Kings 18:12; 2 Kings 2:11). The Spirit carried Ezekiel here and there (Ezekiel 3:14). He carried Christ from the top of the pinnacle of the temple into Galilee (Luke 4:9-14). Through the Spirit, Jesus walked on the sea (Matthew 14:25). The Spirit caught Philip away from the eunuch and carried him as far as Azotus (Acts 8:39-40).

We see that the great God has given us a taste of the power and glory that is in Himself, and how easily it will help us, by permeating us at the resurrection, to act and do like angels. As Christ said, those who will be counted worthy of that world, and of the resurrection from the dead, will not die, but will be equal to the angels (Luke 20:36).

Just as the body by being spiritualized will be as has been explained, so all the service of the body and abilities of the soul must necessarily be infinitely enlarged also. Then *we shall see him as he is* (1 John 3:2), and then we shall know even as we are known (1 Corinthians 13:12).

We shall see him. That is, we will see Christ in His glory – not by revelation only, as we do now, but then face to face, and He wants us with Him for this very purpose (John 17:24). Although John was in the Spirit when he had the vision of Christ, yet it made him fall at His feet as dead (Revelation 1:17). Daniel's vision of Christ involved such a glorious and dominating glory that it turned Daniel's beauty into corruption (Daniel 10:8). At the day of our resurrection, we will be so furnished that, with the eagle, we will be able to look upon the sun in its strength, and we will then see Him as He is, who now is in the light, that no eye has seen, nor can any man see, until that day (1 Timothy 6:16).

We will see into all things. There will not be anything hidden from us. There will not be a saint, a prophet, or any saved soul, small or great, whom we will not then perfectly know. Also, we will see and know all the works of creation, election, and redemption, and all the things of heaven, earth, and hell, even as completely and perfectly as we now know our ABCs. For the Spirit, with whom every cranny of soul and body will be filled, *searcheth all things, yea, the deep things of God* (1 Corinthians 2:10). We see what extraordinary things have been known by the prophets and saints of God, and that was when they only knew *in part* (1 Corinthians 13:9).

Abraham could, by the Spirit, tell to a day how long his descendants would be under persecution in Egypt (Genesis 15:13). Elisha could tell what was done in the king of Assyria's bedchamber (2 Kings 6:12). Ahijah knew Jeroboam's wife as soon, and even before, her feet entered within his door, although he had not seen her (1 Kings 14:1-6).

The prophet of Judah could tell by the Spirit what God would do to Bethel because of the idolatry committed there. He could also point out the man by name who would carry out this work, long before he was born (1 Kings 13:2). Enoch could tell what would be done at the end of the world (Jude 1:14-15). By the Spirit, the prophets, to a detail, prophesied of Christ's birth, His death, His burial, of their giving Him gall and vinegar, of their parting His raiment, and of their piercing His hands and feet (Isaiah 53). They also prophesied of His riding on a donkey (Zechariah 9:9). All this they saw when they spoke of Him (John 12:41). Peter also, although half asleep, could at the very first word call Moses and Elijah by their names when they appeared to Christ in the holy mount (Luke 9:33).

He who doubts these things is very ignorant of the operation of the Spirit of God. If these things have been done, seen, and known by spiritual men while their knowledge has been but *in part*, how will we know, see, and discern *when that which is perfect is come* (1 Corinthians 13:10)! This will happen at the resurrection: *It is raised a spiritual body* (1 Corinthians 15:44).

Conclusion

In a few words, I have shown you the truth of the resurrection of the just, as well as the manner of their rising. If I had judged it convenient, I could have elaborated much on each point, and could have added many more, for the doctrine of the resurrection, no matter how questioned it is by heretics and other erroneous persons, is such a truth, that almost all the Holy Scriptures of God point at it and center in it.

From the beginning of the world, God has shown us that our bodies, as well as our souls, will be with Him in the kingdom of heaven. He has shown us how He will deal with those who are alive at Christ's coming. He has shown us this by His translating of Enoch and by taking him body and soul to Himself (Genesis 5:24; Hebrews 11:5), as well as by taking up Elijah body and soul into heaven in a fiery chariot (2 Kings 2:11).

> From the beginning of the world, God has shown us that our bodies, as well as our souls, will be with Him in the kingdom of heaven.

Secondly, He has often put us in remembrance of the rising of those who are dead at that day. (1) By the faith he gave Abraham concerning the offering of his son, for when he offered him, he believed *that God was able to raise him up, even from the dead; from whence also he received him in a figure* (Hebrews 11:19) – in a figure of the resurrection of Christ for Abraham's justification, and of Abraham's resurrection by Christ at the last day for His glorification. (2) By the faith He gave Joseph concerning his bones, which command the godly Hebrews in Egypt diligently observed, and to that purpose, kept them four hundred years, at last carrying them from Egypt to Canaan, which was a type of our being carried in our body from this world to heaven (Hebrews 11:22).

In addition, how often did God give power to His prophets, servants, and Christ Jesus to raise some who were then dead, and some who had been dead for a long while; and all, no doubt, to put the present generations, as well as the generations yet unborn, in mind of the resurrection of the dead. To this purpose, I ask how the Shunammite's son was raised from the dead (2 Kings 4:32-35). What about the man at the touching of the bones of Elisha (2 Kings 13:20-21)?

These people, along with Lazarus (John 11:39-44), Jairus's daughter (Matthew 9:18-26), Tabitha (Acts 9:40-41), and many others who, after their souls were departed from them (Lazarus had been in his grave four days), were all raised to life again and lived with that very body out of which the soul, at their death, had departed.

Above all, that notable place in Matthew at the resurrection of the Lord Jesus gives us a notable foreword of the resurrection of the just: *And the graves were opened; and many bodies of the saints which slept arose, and came out of the graves after his resurrection, and went into the holy city, and appeared unto many* (Matthew 27:52-53).

When the author to the Hebrews had given us a list of the worthy people of the Old Testament, he said at last, *These all died in faith* (Hebrews 11:13). In the faith of what? That they should lie and rot in their grave eternally? Not at all. That is the faith of Ranters, not of Christians. These worthy people all died in faith that they would rise again, and therefore they considered this world not worth living in, upon unworthy terms, that after death *they might obtain a better resurrection* (Hebrews 11:35).

It is also worth considering what Paul wrote to the Philippians, where he said that he was confident that God, who had begun a good work in them, would *perform it until the day of Jesus Christ* (Philippians 1:6). The *day of Jesus Christ* was not the day of their conversion, for that day had already passed; they were now the children of God. This day of Christ, though, is the same that in other places is called the day when He will come with the sound of the last trump to raise the dead.

You must know that the work of salvation is not at an end with those who are now in heaven, and it never will be until (as I showed you before) their bodies are raised again. As I have said, God has made our bodies the members of Christ, and God does not regard us as thoroughly saved until our bodies are as well redeemed and ransomed out of the grave and death as our souls are from the curse of the law and the dominion of sin.

Although God's saints have felt the power of much of His grace and have had many sweet words fulfilled in their lives, yet one promise will be unfulfilled on their individual person as long as the grave can close her mouth upon them; but, as I said before, when the gates of death open before them and the bars of the grave fall asunder, then that saying will be brought to pass that is written, *Death is swallowed up in victory* (1 Corinthians 15:54). Then they will hear that most pleasant voice, *Awake and sing, ye that dwell in dust: for thy dew is as the dew of herbs, and the earth shall cast out the dead* (Isaiah 26:19). Let us consider these points of the truth of the resurrection of the just and the manner of their rising.

You should know that the time of the rising of these just people will be at the coming of the Lord, for when they arise, or rather, just before they are raised, the Lord Jesus Christ will appear in the clouds in flaming fire with His mighty angels (2 Thessalonians 1:7-8). The effect of this appearing will be the rising of the dead, etc. *For the Lord himself shall descend from heaven with a shout, with the voice of the archangel, and with the trump of God: and the dead shall rise* (1 Thessalonians 4:16; see also 1 Corinthians 15:52).

Now at the time of the Lord's coming, there will be found alive in the world both saints and sinners. As for the saints who will then be found alive, as soon as all the saints are raised out of their graves, they will not die, but will be changed and swallowed up by incorruption, immortality, and glory. They will have the soul-spiritual transformation just as the raised saints will have. As Paul wrote, *We shall not all [die, or] sleep, but we shall all be changed, in a moment, in the twinkling of an eye, at the last trump: for the trumpet shall sound, and the dead shall be raised incorruptible, and we shall be changed*

(1 Corinthians 15:51-52), and *The Lord himself shall descend from heaven with a shout, with the voice of the archangel, and with the trump of God: and the dead in Christ shall rise first: then we which are alive and remain shall be caught up together with them in the clouds, to meet the Lord in the air: and so shall we ever be with the Lord* (1 Thessalonians 4:16-17). Paul also writes that He *shall judge the quick and the dead at his appearing and his kingdom* (2 Timothy 4:1).

When the saints who sleep will be raised incorruptible, powerful, glorious, and spiritual, and also those who then will be found alive are made like them, then immediately, before the unjust are raised, the saints will appear before the judgment seat of the Lord Jesus Christ to give an account there to their Lord, the Judge, of all things they have done, and to receive a reward for their good according to their labor.

They will rise before the wicked, they themselves being the proper children of the resurrection. That is, they are those who must have all the glory of it, both as to preeminence and sweetness, and therefore when they rise, they are said to rise from the dead, for in their rising, they leave the reprobate world behind them (Luke 20:35-36; Acts 3:15; 4:10; 13:30; John 12:1, 9, 17). It must be so, because also the saints will have given their account and will be set upon the throne with Christ as kings and princes with Him to judge the world when those of the wicked world are raised. The saints will judge the world; they will judge angels – yes, and they will sit upon the thrones of judgment to do it (1 Corinthians 6:2-3; Psalm 122:5).

> The saints will rise before the wicked, they themselves being the proper children of the resurrection.

Next, we come to the examination the just must undergo, as well as the account they must give to the Lord, the Judge.

The Judgment of the Just

As you have heard, when the saints are raised, they must in general give an account of all things that they have done while they were in the world – of all things, whether they are good or bad.

First, saints must give an account of all their bad.

Observe, however, that this is not done under the consideration of vagabonds, slaves, and sinners, but as sons, stewards, and servants of the Lord Jesus. It is evident that this will be so from various places in the Holy Scriptures.

1. Paul says that the saints *shall all stand before the judgment seat of Christ. For it is written, As I live, saith the Lord, every knee shall bow to me, and every tongue shall confess to God. So then every one of us shall give account of himself to God* (Romans 14:10-12). Paul also wrote, *Wherefore we labour, that, whether present or absent, we may be accepted of him. For we must all appear before the judgment seat of Christ; that every one [of us] may receive the things done in his body, according to what he hath done, whether it be good or bad* (2 Corinthians 5:9-10).

It is true that God loves His people, but He does not love

their sins, nor anything they do, even if they do it with the greatest zeal for Him, if the person is contrary to His Word. Just as truly as God will give a reward to His saints and children for all that they have indeed done well, so truly will He at this day distinguish their good and bad; and when both are manifest by the righteous judgment of Christ, He will burn up their bad, with all their labor, travel, and efforts in it for ever. He can tell how to save His people, and yet *take vengeance on their inventions* (Psalm 99:8).

This is a remarkable passage in the third chapter of Paul's epistle to the Corinthians:

> *If any man build upon this foundation [Christ]*
> *gold, silver, precious stones, wood, hay, stubble;*
> *every man's work shall be made manifest: for the*
> *day shall declare it, because it shall be revealed*
> *by fire; and the fire shall try every man's work of*
> *what sort it is. If any man's work abide which he*
> *hath built thereupon, he shall receive a reward.*
> *If any man's work shall be burned, he shall suffer*
> *loss; but he himself shall be saved; yet so as by fire.*
> (1 Corinthians 3:12-15)

Now observe:

1. As I said before, the foundation is Jesus Christ (1 Corinthians 3:11).

2. The gold, silver, and precious stones that are said here to be built upon Him are all that is done in faith and love, according to the Word, that the saints are found doing for His sake in the world (1 Peter 1:7; Revelation 3:18).

3. To build wood, hay, and stubble on Him is to build human inventions and carnal ordinances together with

what is right in itself, establishing them still on God and His allowance.

4. The fire that you read of here is the pure Word and Law of God (Jeremiah 23:29; John 12:48).

5. The day that you read of here is the day of Christ's coming in judgment to reveal the *hidden things of darkness*, and to *make manifest the counsels of the heart* (1 Corinthians 4:5).

6. On that day, the gold, silver, precious stones, wood, hay, and stubble of everyone will be tested by this fire so that it may be made clear of what sort it is. The wind, rain, and floods beat now as fiercely against the house upon the rock as against that on the sand (Luke 6:48-49).

Notice also:

1. The apostle Paul speaks here of the saved, not of the reprobate: *He himself shall be saved.*

2. This saved man may have wood, hay, and stubble; that is, he may have things that will not endure the testing.

3. Neither this man's goodness, nor yet God's love to him, will hinder all his wood, hay, or stubble from being tested: *Every man's work shall be manifest: . . . the fire shall try every man's work, of what sort it is.*

4. Consequently, a good man will see all his wood, hay, and stubble burnt up in the testing before his face.

5. That good man will then suffer loss, or the loss of all things that are not then according to the Word of God. *If any man's works shall be burned, he shall suffer loss; but he himself shall be saved; yet so as by fire* (1 Corinthians 3:15). That is, all that he has ever done will be tested in accordance with the Word of God.

From all this, it must be unavoidably concluded that the whole body of the elect must give an account to their Lord for all things they have done, whether good or bad, and that He will destroy all their bad with the purity of His Word, along with all their effort, travel, and labor that they have spent in regard to it. I am convinced that there are now many things done by the best of saints that they will then gladly renounce and be ashamed of – yes, things that they have done and still do with great devotion. Alas, what shocking things some of the saints, in their devotion, attribute to God, consider Him the author of these things, think that He encourages them to do these things, and even gives them His presence in the performance of them! Yes, and as they create many untruths and attribute many unbiblical acts and beliefs to Him, so they die in the same opinion and never in this world arrive at the sight of their evil and ignorance herein.[2]

The judgment day is the main time in which everything will be set in its proper place. That which is of God will be put in its place, and that which is not will then be disclosed and made clear. *In many things we offend all* (James 3:2), and then we will see the many offenses we have committed, and will ourselves judge them as they are.

In this world, the Christian is so candid a creature that if you take him when he is not under some great temptation, he will aptly confess to his God, before all men, how he has sinned and transgressed against his Father. He will fall down at the

---

2   This is a terrible state of delusion – to imagine that God is the author of abhorrent things, such as worshipping a wafer, or appealing to a priest to forgive sins – and then thinking that a holy God urges them to do these things and even approves of them by His presence! Christian, take care that you do not receive any doctrine, nor conform to any practice in religion, without prayerful investigation and a *thus saith the Lord* for its approval (George Offor, Editor).

feet of God and cry, "You are righteous, for I have sinned; and You are gracious, so that despite my sin, You would save me."

If the Christian is so simple and plain-hearted with God in the days of his imperfection, when he is accompanied with many infirmities and temptations, how freely will he confess and acknowledge his misdeeds when he comes before his Lord and Savior completely free of all temptation and imperfection! *As I live, saith the Lord, every knee shall bow to me, and every tongue shall confess to God* (Romans 14:11; see also Philippians 2:10-11). Every knee will bow and will reverence God the Creator and Christ the Redeemer of the world. Every tongue will confess that God's will alone should have been obeyed by them in all things. They (the saints) will also confess, and will do so most naturally and freely, in how many things they were deceived, mistaken, deceived, and drawn aside in their intended devotion and honor to God.

2. Take notice that in this day, when the saints are giving an account for their evil before their Savior and Judge, they will not then, as now, at the remembrance and confession of sin, be filled with the guilt, confusion, and shame that now attends their souls through the weakness of faith. Neither will they in the least be grieved or offended that before the angels and the rest of their holy brethren, God has laid open their infirmities from the least and first to the biggest and last. They will not be grieved or offended for the following reasons:

1. They will now more perfectly than ever see that the God to whom they confess everything loves them and frees them from all their sins and shortcomings, even when and before they confess and acknowledge them to Him. They will have their souls so full of the delightful joys of the life and glory that they are then in that they will be swallowed up of it in such a measure and manner that

neither fear, nor guilt, nor confusion can come near them or touch them. Their Judge is their Savior, their Husband, and their Head, who, although He will bring every one of them to judgment for all things, yet He will forever keep them out of condemnation and anything that leans that way. *Perfect love casteth out fear* (1 John 4:18), even while we are here. It will be much more then, when we are with our Savior, our Jesus, being *passed from death unto life* (John 5:24).

2. The saints in that day will have their hearts and souls so wrapped up in the pleasure of God their Savior that it will be their delight to see all things, even those things that were once near and dear unto them, perish if they were not according to His Word and will. *Thy will be done* is always to be our language here (Matthew 6:10). However, to delight to see it done in all things, even if it results in the destruction of what we love, and to delight to see it done in the height and perfection of delight, will not happen fully until we get to heaven, or when the Lord will come to judge the world.

3. The single purpose for the saints giving an account at the day of God will not just be for the vindication of the righteousness, holiness, and purity of the Word, nor will it center only in the manifestation of the knowledge and heart-discerning nature of Christ (although both these will be in it [Revelation 2:22-23]), but their very remembrances and sight of the vanity and sin that they have done while here will both point to and heighten the tender affections of their God unto them, and will also increase their joy and sweetness of soul and the clinging of heart to their God.

48

While here, saints are gratefully aware that the sense of sin and the assurance of pardon will make wonderful work in their poor hearts. What emotion without guilt, what humility without humiliation, and what a sight of the creature's nothingness, yet without fear, will this sense of sin work in the soul! The sweetest frame of mind, the most heart-endearing disposition that a Christian can possibly get into while in this world, is to have a warm sight of sin and a Savior upon the heart at the same time. The soul then weeps, not out of fear and through torment, but by virtue of constraining grace and mercy. It is at this very time, so far from distress of heart by reason of the sight of its wickedness, that it is driven into joy by reason of the love and mercy that is mingled with the sense of sin in the soul.

The heart has not seen as much of the power of mercy as now, nor of the virtue, value, and excellency of Christ in all His roles as now. Never before has the tongue been as sweetly enlarged to proclaim and commend grace as now. It is now when Christ *shall come to be glorified in his saints, and to be admired in all them that believe* (2 Thessalonians 1:10).

Wherefore, although the saints receive the forgiveness of sins in this life by faith, and so are passed from death to life, yet Christ Jesus and God His Father will have every one of these sins considered again and brought fresh upon the stage in the day of judgment so that they may see and be sensible forever what grace and mercy has laid hold upon them. I take this to be the reason for that remarkable saying of the apostle Peter:

> *Repent ye therefore, and be converted, that your sins may be blotted out, when the times of refreshing shall come from the presence of the Lord; and he shall send Jesus Christ, which before was preached unto you: whom the heaven must receive until the times of restitution of all things, which God hath*

*spoken by the mouth of all his holy prophets since
the world began.* (Acts 3:19-21)

If a sense of some sin (for who sees all? [Psalm 19:12]) and a
sight of the love of God will so work upon the spirit of the godly
here, then what will a sight of all sin do when together with it
they are personally present with their Lord and Savior?

If a sight of some sins with a possibility of forgiveness will
make the heart love, reverence, and fear with guiltless and
heart-affecting fears, then what will a
general sight of all sin along with an
eternal release and forgiveness from
them work on the heart of the saint
forever?

> What will a general sight of all sin along with an eternal release and forgiveness from them work on the heart of the saint forever?

Yes, if a sight of sin and the love of
God will make such work in that soul
where there is still unbelief, blindness,
mistrust, and forgetfulness, then what will a sight of sin do in
that person who is swallowed up in love, who is sinless and
temptationless, and who has all the capabilities of soul and body
strained by love and grace to the highest point of perfection
that is possible to be enjoyed and possessed in glory?

Oh, the wisdom and goodness of God, that He in that day
would so inquire about the worst of our things, even those
that naturally tend to sink us and condemn us, for our great
advantage! Indeed, *All things work together for good to them
that love God* (Romans 8:28). Those sins that brought a curse
upon the whole world, that spilt the heart-blood of our dearest
Savior, and that laid His tender soul under the fiery wrath of
God, will, by His wisdom and love, contribute to the exalta-
tion of His grace and the stirring up of our affections to Him
forever and ever (Revelation 5:9-14).

It will not be so with demons. It will not be this way with

reprobates. Only the saved have this privilege special to themselves. Wherefore, to vary a little from the matter in hand: will God make use of sin, even though we give account for it, that will in this manner work for our advantage? Let saints, then, also make that advantage of their sin so as to glorify God by it, which is to be done, not by saying, *Let us do evil, that good may come* (Romans 3:8), or Let us sin so *that grace may abound* (Romans 6:1), but by taking occasion by the sin that is past to set the crown upon the head of Christ for our justification, continually looking upon it so as to drive us to cling close to the Lord Jesus, to grace and mercy through Him, and to keep us humble forever under all His kindness and conduct to us.

After having given account for all their evil, and having confessed to God's glory how they fell short and did not obey and live the truth in this or that or other areas, and having received their eternal pardon from the Lord and Judge in the sight of both angels and saints, then the Lord Jesus will immediately ask about all the good that they did.

Second, saints must give an account of all the good and holy actions and deeds they did in the world.

Here all things will be calculated, from the very first good thing that was done by Adam or Abel, to the last that will happen to be done in the world. The good of all the holy prophets, of all apostles, pastors, teachers, and helpers in the church will also here be brought forth and brought to light, along with all the good behavior, attitudes, and demeanors of heads of families, of parents, of children, of employees, of neighbors, or whatever good thing anyone does. I will attempt to be general and brief.

1. There will be a reward for all who have sincerely labored in the Word and doctrine. There will be a recompense for all the souls they have saved by their word, and watered by the same. Now will Paul the planter, and Apollos the waterer, along with every one of their companions, receive the reward that is according to their works (1 Corinthians 3:6-8).

All the preaching, praying, watching, and labor you have done in working to bring people from Satan to God will then be rewarded with shining glory. There is not a soul you have converted to the Lord Jesus, nor a soul you have comforted, strengthened, or helped by your wholesome counsel, admonition, and comfortable speech, that will not be as a pearl in that crown *which the Lord, the righteous judge, shall give [you] at that day* (2 Timothy 4:7-8).

That is, it will be rewarded if you have done it willingly, delighting to lift up the name of God among people, and if you have done it with love and with a desire for the salvation of sinners; otherwise you will only have your labor for your efforts, and nothing more. *If I do this thing willingly, I have a reward: but if against my will, a dispensation of the gospel is committed unto me* (1 Corinthians 9:17; see also Philippians 1:15). However, if you do it graciously, then a reward follows: *For what is our hope, or joy, or crown of rejoicing? Are not even ye in the presence of our Lord Jesus Christ at his coming? For ye are our glory and joy* (1 Thessalonians 2:19-20).

Let him therefore whom Christ has put into His harvest take comfort in the midst of all his sorrow. Let him know that God acknowledges that he who converts a sinner *from the error of his way* saves that soul from death and covers *a multitude of sins* (James 5:20). Therefore, labor to convert, labor to water, labor to build up, and labor to *feed the flock of God which is among you, taking the oversight thereof, not by constraint, but willingly; not for filthy lucre, but of a ready mind. . . . And when the chief Shepherd shall appear, ye shall receive a crown of glory that fadeth not away* (1 Peter 5:2, 4).

2. Just as the ministers of Christ's gospel will be rewarded at this day, so will also those more private saints, with tender affection and love, be rewarded for all their work and labor of love that they have shown in the name of Christ in ministering to His saints and suffering for His sake (Hebrews 6:10). *Whatsoever good thing any man doeth, the same shall he receive of the Lord, whether he be bond or free* (Ephesians 6:8).

How little do the people of God consider how abundantly and thoroughly God will acknowledge and reward all the good and holy acts of His people on that day! Every bit, every drop, every word, and every night's lodging, even if only a piece of straw, will be rewarded in that day before men and angels. Jesus said, *Whosoever shall give to drink unto one of these little ones a cup of cold water only in the name of a disciple, verily I say unto you, he shall in no wise lose his [a disciple's] reward*

> How little do the people of God consider how abundantly God will acknowledge and reward all the good and holy acts of His people on that day!

(Matthew 10:42). Therefore, *when thou makest a feast,* Jesus said, *call the poor, the maimed, the lame, the blind: and thou shalt be blessed; for they cannot recompense thee: for thou shalt be recompensed at the resurrection of the just* (Luke 14:13-14).

If there is any repentance among the godly on that day, it will be because the Lord Jesus, in His person, body, and Word, was not more loved, honored, cared for, and provided for by them when they were in this world. It will be pleasing to all to see the Lord Jesus then take notice of every widow's mite. He will call to mind even all those acts of mercy and kindness that you have shown to Him when you were among men. He will remember, point out, and proclaim before angels and saints those very acts of yours that you have either forgotten or, through humility, will not at that day consider worth mentioning. He will count them up so fast and so fully that you will cry, "Lord, when did I do this, and when did I do that?"

> When saw we thee an hungered, and fed thee? or
> thirsty, and gave thee drink? When saw we thee a
> stranger, and took thee in? or naked, and clothed
> thee? Or when saw we thee sick, or in prison, and
> came unto thee? And the King shall answer and say
> unto them, Verily I say unto you, inasmuch as ye
> have done it unto one of the least of these my breth-
> ren, ye have done it unto me. (Matthew 25:37-40)

The good works of some are manifest beforehand; and they that are otherwise cannot be hid (1 Timothy 5:25). "Whatever you have done to one of the least of these My brethren, you have done it unto Me. I felt the nourishment of your food and the warmth of your fleece. I remember your loving and holy visits when My poor members were sick and in prison and such. When they were strangers and wanderers in the world, you took them in. *Well done, thou good and faithful servant; . . . enter thou into the joy of thy Lord*" (Matthew 25:21-23, 34-47).

3. There also will be a reward for all that hardship and Christian enduring of affliction that you have met with for your Lord while you were in the world. Christ will begin from the great-est suffering even to the least, and will bestow a reward on them all. From the blood of the suffering saint to the loss of a hair – nothing will go unrewarded (Hebrews 11:36-40; 2 Corinthians 8:8-14). *For our light affliction, which is but for a moment, worketh for us a far more exceeding and eternal weight of glory* (2 Corinthians 4:17).

We can see in the Scriptures how God has recorded the suf-ferings of His people, and also how He has promised to reward them. *Blessed are they which are persecuted for righteousness' sake: for theirs is the kingdom of heaven. Blessed are ye, when men shall revile you, and persecute you, and shall say all manner of evil against you falsely, for my sake. Rejoice [leap for joy], and be exceeding glad: for great is your reward in heaven* (Matthew 5:11-12; Luke 6:22-23). *And every one that hath forsaken houses, or brethren, or sisters, or father, or mother, or wife, or children, or lands, for my name's sake, shall receive an hundredfold, and shall inherit everlasting life* (Matthew 19:29).

4. On that day there is also a reward for all the more secret and more secluded works of Christianity.

1. There is not now one act of faith in your soul, either upon Christ or against the devil and the Antichrist, that will not on this day be disclosed and praised, honored and glorified in the face of heaven (1 Peter 1:7).

> There is not one act of faith in your soul that will not on this day be honored and glorified in the face of heaven

2. There is not one groan to God in secret against your own lusts and for more grace, light, Spirit, sanctification, and strength to go through this world like a Christian that will not be rewarded openly at the coming of Christ (Matthew 6:6).

3. Not one tear has dropped from your tender eye against your lusts, the love of this world, or for more communion with Jesus Christ that is not now in the bottle of God. It will then bring forth such abundance of reward that it will return upon you with abundance of increase. *Blessed are ye that weep now: for ye shall laugh* (Luke 6:21). *Thou tellest my wanderings: put thou my tears into thy bottle; are they not in thy book?* (Psalm 56:8). *They that sow in tears shall reap in joy. He that goeth forth and weepeth,*

bearing precious seed, shall doubtless come again with rejoicing, bringing his sheaves with him (Psalm 126:5-6).

Having thus briefly shown you something about the resurrection of the saints, and that they will give an account to their Lord at His coming, both for burning up what was not according to the truth, and rewarding them for all their good, I will now briefly discuss how the saints will be rewarded.

The Reward of the Just

First, when those who will be found in the day of their resurrection have all their good things brought up on display, then will be found the people most laborious for God while they were here. At that day, they will enjoy the greatest portion of God, or will most rejoice in and share in the glory of the Godhead then, for that is the portion of saints in general (Lamentations 3:24; Romans 8:17).

Why will he who does the most for God in this world enjoy the most of Him in that world which is to come? It is because by doing and acting, the heart and every ability of the soul is enlarged and more capable, whereby more room is made for glory. Every vessel of glory will at that day be full of glory, but not all will be capable of containing the same measure of that glory. If they would have it imparted to them, they would not be able to bear it, for there is *an eternal weight of glory* that saints will then enjoy (2 Corinthians 4:17), and every vessel must be filled at that day – that is, each vessel must have its heavenly capacity of it.

All Christians do not have the same enjoyment of God in this life, and they would not all be able to bear it if they had it (1 Corinthians 3:2). But those Christians who are most laborious for God in this world already have most of Him in their souls, and that is not just because diligence in God's ways is the means whereby God communicates Himself, but it is also because by that means the senses are made more strong and are able, by reason of use, to understand God and to discern both good and evil (Hebrews 5:13-14). To him who has, to him shall be given, and he shall have more abundance (Matthew 13:11-12).

> He said therefore, A certain nobleman went into a far country to receive for himself a kingdom, and to return. And he called his ten servants, and delivered them ten pounds, and said unto them, Occupy till I come.
>
> But his citizens hated him, and sent a message after him, saying, We will not have this man to reign over us.
>
> And it came to pass, that when he was returned, having received the kingdom, then he commanded these servants to be called unto him, to whom he had given the money, that he might know how much every man had gained by trading.
>
> Then came the first, saying, Lord, thy pound hath gained ten pounds.
>
> And he said unto him, Well, thou good servant: because thou hast been faithful in a very little, have thou authority over ten cities.
>
> And the second came, saying, Lord, thy pound hath gained five pounds.
>
> And he said likewise to him, Be thou also over five cities. (Luke 19:12-19)

Often, he who is best raised in his youth is best able to manage most when he is a man concerning the things of this life (Daniel 1:3-4). Always, though, he who is best raised and who is most in the presence of God, and who so lives for Him the most here, he is the one who will be best able to enjoy the most of God in the kingdom of heaven.

It is noticeable that Paul said, *Our light affliction, which is but for a moment, worketh for us a far more exceeding and eternal weight of glory* (2 Corinthians 4:17). Our afflictions do this, not only because there is laid up a reward for the afflicted according to the measure of affliction, but because affliction, along with every service of God, makes the heart more deep, more genuine, more knowing, and more profound – and so is more able to hold, contain, and bear more. *It is good for me that I have been afflicted; that I might learn thy statutes* (Psalm 119:71). *Every man shall receive his own reward according to his own labour* (1 Corinthians 3:8).

This is the reason for such sayings as *Laying up in store for themselves a good foundation against the time to come, that they may lay hold on eternal life* (1 Timothy 6:19). This eternal life is not the matter of our justification from sin in the sight of God, for that is done freely by grace through faith in Christ's blood (but here the apostle Paul speaks of giving of alms), but it is the same that in another place he calls the *far more exceeding and eternal weight of glory* (2 Corinthians 4:17). This is the reason that in his stirring them up to be diligent in good works, Paul tells them that he does not exhort them to it because he wanted anything for himself, but because he desired *fruit that may abound to [their] account* (Philippians 4:17). He says in another place, *Beloved brethren, be ye steadfast, unmoveable, always abounding in the work of the Lord, forasmuch as ye know that your labour is not in vain in the Lord* (1 Corinthians 15:58).

This is why I say that the reward that the saints will have on that day for all the good they have done is the enjoyment of God according to their works, even though they will be freely justified and glorified without works.

Second, as the enjoyment of God at that day will be to the saints according to their works and words and actions (I am not speaking now of justification from sin), so will their praise and commendations at that day be according to the same, and both of them will result in their degrees of glory. As God will thereby glorify us by communicating Himself unto us at that day, so will He also, to add all things that may provide glory in every way, cause to be proclaimed in the face of heaven and in the presence of all the holy angels everything that has been done by us for God, His ways, and His people while we have been here. *There is nothing covered, that shall not be revealed; neither hid, that shall not be known. Whatsoever ye have spoken in darkness shall be heard in the light; and that which ye have spoken in the ear in closets shall be proclaimed upon the housetops* (Luke 12:2-3). Again, Jesus said, *Whosoever therefore shall confess me before men, him will I confess also before my Father which is in heaven* (Matthew 10:32).

He of whom Christ is ashamed when He comes in His glory and in the glory of the holy angels will then lie under inconceivable disgrace, shame, dishonor, and contempt. Yet he whom Christ will confess, acknowledge, commend, and praise at that day will have very great dignity, honor, and renown, for *then shall every man have praise of God* – that is, according to his works (1 Corinthians 4:5).

In that day, Christ will proclaim before you and all others

what you have done, what you have suffered, what you have acknowledged, and what you have endured for His name (Mark 8:38): "This is someone who forsook his goods, his relations, his country, and his life for Me. This is the man who overcame the flatteries, threats, allurements, and enticements of a whole world for Me. Behold, he is *an Israelite indeed* [John 1:47], the top man in his generation. There is *none like him in all the earth* [Job 1:8]."

When King Ahasuerus understood how much good Mordecai the Jew had done to and for him, he commanded that the royal apparel and the crown, with the horse that the king rode on, should be given to him, and that with that crown, clothing, and horse, he should be led through the city in the presence of all his nobles, and that proclamation should be made before him: *Thus shall it be done unto the man whom the king delighteth to honour* (Esther 6:9-11).

> Those people who will make it their business to honor Jesus in the day of their temptation, He will make it His business to honor them in the day of His glorification.

Ahasuerus in this was an example to the children of God of how kindly God will take all their labor and service of love, and how He will honor and dignify the same. As Christ saith:

> *Let your loins be girded about, and your lights burning; and ye yourselves like unto men that wait for their lord, when he will return from the wedding; that when he cometh and knocketh, they may open unto him immediately. Blessed are those servants, whom the lord when he cometh shall find watching: verily I say unto you, that he shall gird himself, and make them sit down to meat, and will come forth and serve them.* (Luke 12:35-37)

The meaning is that for those people who will make it their business to honor the Lord Jesus Christ in the day of their temptation, He will make it His business to honor and glorify them in the day of His glorification. *Verily, I say unto you, that he shall gird himself, and make them sit down to meat, and will come forth and serve them* (Luke 12:37). *If any man serve me, him will my Father honour* (John 12:26). It has been God's way in this world to proclaim the acts and deeds of His saints in His Word before all in this world, and He will do it in that which is to come (Mark 14:9; Revelation 3:4; 14:1-6).

Third, another thing that will be still added to the glory of the saints in the kingdom of their Savior at His coming is that every one of them will then have his throne and place of degree on Christ's right hand, and on His left, in His glorious kingdom, according to the relation they have in Christ as the members of His body. Just as Christ will have a special eye on us and a tender and affectionate heart to recompense to the full every good thing that anyone does for His name in this world, so also He will have as much regard that every member of His body has the place and state that is pleasing for every such member.

When the mother of Zebedee's children petitioned our Savior that He would grant to her that her two sons might sit the one on His right hand and the other on His left in His kingdom, although He did not grant her the request for her children, yet He affirmed that there would be places of degrees and honor in heaven. He answered, *To sit on my right hand, and on my left, is not mine to give, but it shall be given to them for whom it is prepared of my Father* (Matthew 20:23). In the temple, there were bigger and smaller rooms, higher and lower, more inward and more outward. These rooms were types of the mansions that our Lord, when He went away, told us that He was going to prepare for us: *In my Father's house are many mansions: if it were not so, I would have told you. I go to prepare a place for you* (John 14:2).

The foot here will not have the place prepared for the eye, nor will the hand have that which is prepared for the ear, but every person will have his own place in the body of Christ, along with the glory also prepared for such a relation. Order is pleasing in earth, and it is much more pleasing in the kingdom of the God of order, in heaven, where all things will be done in their utmost perfections.

This is where Enoch, Noah, Abraham, Moses, Joshua, David, and the prophets each have his place according to the degree of Old Testament saints. As God said to Daniel, *Go thou thy way till the end be: for thou shalt rest, and stand in thy lot at the end of the days* (Daniel 12:13). This is also where Peter, Paul, Timothy, and all the other church officers have their place and heavenly state, according as God has set them in the church in the New Testament. As Paul said of the deacons, *They that have used the office of a deacon well, purchase to themselves a good degree, and great boldness in the faith which is in Christ Jesus* (1 Timothy 3:13).

It is the same with all other saints of whatever rank, quality, or place they have in the body of Christ. Every follower of Jesus will have his state, his heavenly state, according as he stands in the body. As Paul said, since those members who are most feeble are necessary, to them will be given *more abundant honour* (1 Corinthians 12:22-23).

Of this heavenly order in the kingdom of Christ, when His saints are risen from the dead, Solomon was a notable type in his family, and among his servants and officers, who kept such exactness in the famous order in which he had placed all about him, that it amazed and confounded beholders. *When the queen of Sheba had seen the wisdom of Solomon, and the house that he had built, and the meat of his table, and the sitting of his servants, and the attendance of his ministers, and their apparel; his cupbearers also, and their apparel; and his ascent by which he went up into the house of the Lord, there was no more spirit in her* (2 Chronicles 9:3-4). *Glorious things are spoken of thee, O city of God* (Psalm 87:3).

The Resurrection of the Wicked

I now come to the second part of the text, that there will be a resurrection of the wicked. *There shall be a resurrection of the dead, both of the just and unjust* (Acts 24:15). As the just go before the unjust in name and dignity and honor, so in the last day they will go before them in the resurrection.

After the saints have thus risen out of their graves, given their accounts to God, received their glory, and are set upon the thrones, *for there are set thrones of judgment, the thrones of the house of David* (Psalm 122:5), after all of them are in their royal apparel with crowns of glory, every one displaying the person of a king, then the unjust will come out of their graves to receive their judgment for what they have done in the body. As Paul said, *We must all appear before the judgment seat of Christ, that every one* (both saints and sinners) *may receive the things done in the body, according to that he hath done, whether it be good or bad* (2 Corinthians 5:10).

Now, because I desire to prove by the Word whatever I want others to receive as truth, therefore I will in a few points prove the resurrection of the wicked.

First, it is evident that the wicked will rise based upon the very terms and names that are then applied to them, which are the very same names that they were referred to when they lived in this world. They are called the heathen, the nations, the world, the wicked, and those who do iniquity. They are called men and women of Sodom, Sidon, Bethsaida, Capernaum, and Tyre (Luke 10:12-16). The men of Nineveh and the queen of the south will rise up in the judgment (Matthew 12:41-42). It will be more tolerable for Sodom in the day of judgment than for other sinners who have resisted more light (Matthew 11:21-24). *The heavens and the earth, which are now, . . . are kept in store, reserved unto fire against the day of judgment and perdition of ungodly men* (2 Peter 3:7; see also Joel 3:12-14).

These terms, or names, are not given to the *spirits* of the wicked only, but are given to them as consisting of body and soul. Further, Christ tells His adversaries, after they had apprehended Him and shamefully entreated Him, that they would see Him sit on the right hand of power and coming in the clouds of heaven (Matthew 25:31; 26:64; Jude 1:14-15). John also testifies to this: *Behold, he cometh with clouds; and every eye shall see him, and they also which pierced him: and all kindreds of the earth shall wail because of him* (Revelation 1:7).

None of these sayings are yet fulfilled, and they will not be fulfilled until His second coming. Although many of the Jews did see Him when He was hanging upon the cross, yet He was not then coming in the clouds of heaven, neither then did all kindreds of the earth wail because of Him. No, this is reserved until He comes to judge the world, for then the ungodly would gladly creep into the most invincible rock or mountain under heaven to hide themselves from His face and the majesty of His heavenly presence (Revelation 6:14-17).

Therefore, so that this may be brought to pass, there will be *a resurrection of the dead, both of the just and unjust.* For though a belief of no resurrection may now lull people asleep in security and impiety, yet the Lord will awaken them when He comes. He will not only awaken them out of their security, but out of their graves, to their doom, that they may receive the proper recompense for their transgression that is due to them.

Second, the body of the ungodly must arise out of the grave on that day because that body and its soul, while they lived in the world, were copartners in their lusts and wickedness. *The* LORD *is a God of knowledge, and by him actions are weighed* (1 Samuel 2:3). He will therefore *bring every work into judgment, with every secret thing* (Ecclesiastes 12:14). Just as He will bring every work into judgment, so will He also bring the worker of that work into judgment, even *the dead, small and great* (Revelation 20:12).

God does not lay the punishment where the fault is not, neither does He punish a part of the condemned for the whole. *With righteousness shall he judge the world, and the people with equity* (Psalm 98:9). *Shall not the Judge of all the earth do right?* (Genesis 18:25). Therefore, as the body was copartner with the soul in sinning, so shall every person *receive the things done in his body* according to what he has done (2 Corinthians 5:10). Jesus says in another place, *Behold, I come quickly; and my reward is with me, to give every man according as his work shall be* (Revelation 22:12). Therefore, we see that there will be *a resurrection of the dead, both of the just and unjust.*

> God does not lay the punishment where the fault is not, neither does He punish a part of the condemned for the whole.

Third, the body of the wicked must rise again because just as the whole man of the just is the vessel of mercy and glory, so the whole man of the unjust is the vessel of wrath and destruction. Paul said, *In a great house there are not only vessels of* *gold and of silver, but also of wood and of earth; and some to honour, and some to dishonour* (2 Timothy 2:20). Now, as he shows us, these vessels to honor are good men, and the vessels to dishonor are the bad (2 Timothy 2:21). Now as these vessels to dishonor are called the vessels of wrath, so it is said that God, with much long-suffering, allows them to be *fitted to destruction* (Romans 9:22).

Paul also shows us how they are further prepared for destruction where he says, *After thy hardness and impenitent heart [you] treasure up unto thyself wrath against the day of wrath and revelation of the righteous judgment of God* (Romans 2:5). James says that these treasures of wickedness are treasures *heaped . . . together for the last days* (which is the time of judgment). Notice that he says that they will eat their flesh *as it were fire* (James 5:2-3).

Now then, since their bodies are the vessels of the wrath of God, since they must be possessed with this wrath at the last day, and since their flesh must by it be eaten, it is evident that their bodies must rise again out of their graves and appear before the judgment seat; for it is from there that each of them must go with his full burden to their long and eternal home *where their worm dieth not, and the fire is not quenched* (Mark 9:48).

Fourth, the severity of the hand of God toward His children, along with His patience toward His enemies, clearly communicates a resurrection of the ungodly so that they may receive the reward for their wickedness that they have committed in this world. We know that while the eyes of the wicked start out *with fatness*, the godly are plagued *all the day long*, and are *chastened every morning* (Psalm 73:3-15). Therefore, it is evident that the place and time of the punishment of the ungodly is in another world.

If *judgment must begin at the house of God . . . , what shall* the end be of them that obey not the gospel of God? And if the righteous scarcely be saved, where shall the ungodly and the sinner appear? (1 Peter 4:17-18). Alas, poor creatures! They now plot against the righteous and gnash upon them with their teeth, but the LORD shall laugh at him, for he seeth that his day is coming (Psalm 37:13). As God's Word says, the wicked is reserved, or let alone in his wickedness, to the day of destruction, and shall then be brought forth to the day of wrath, although in the meantime, he will be brought to the grave, and shall remain in the tomb (Job 21:30-32). As Peter says, The Lord knoweth how to deliver the godly out of temptations, and to reserve the unjust unto the day of judgment to be punished (2 Peter 2:9). Jude says that to them is reserved the blackness of darkness for ever (Jude 1:13). The punishment of the ungodly is reserved until the day of judgment, which will be the time of their resurrection.

Observe the following points:

1. The wicked must be punished.

2. The time of their punishment is not now, but at the day of judgment.

3. This day of judgment must be the same as the time of the resurrection of the dead at the end of this world. As therefore the tares are gathered and burned in the fire; so shall it be in the end of this world. The Son of man shall send forth his angels, and they shall gather out of his kingdom all things that offend, and them which do iniquity; and shall cast them into a furnace of fire: there shall be wailing and gnashing of teeth (Matthew 13:40-42). There will then be a resurrection of the dead, both of the just and unjust.

4. The sovereignty of the Lord Jesus over all creatures plainly foretells a resurrection of the bad, as well as of the good. Indeed, the unjust will not arise by virtue of any standing they have in relation to the Lord Jesus, as the saints

will, yet because all are delivered into His hand, and He is the sovereign Lord over them, therefore, by an act of His sovereign power, those who are ungodly will arise.

This is Christ's own argument: *The Father judgeth no man, but hath committed all judgment unto the Son* (John 5:22). That is, they give their account to Him and fall before him as their sovereign Lord, even as they honor the Father, and the Father has given Jesus authority to carry out judgment also, because He is the Son of man. Then He adds, *Marvel not at this: for the hour is coming, in the which all that are in the graves shall hear his voice, and shall come forth; they that have done good, unto the resurrection of life; and they that have done evil, unto the resurrection of damnation* (John 5:28-29). Paul also argues from this perspective, saying, *For to this end Christ both died, and rose, and revived, that he might be Lord both of the dead and living.* Then he adds, *We shall all stand before the judgment seat of Christ* (Romans 14:9-10).

Please pay attention to these words. Jesus Christ by His death and resurrection not only purchased grace and remission of sins for His elect with their eternal glory, but by this He also was granted by the Father to be Lord and head over all things, whether they are things in heaven, things on earth, or things under the earth. Jesus said, *All power is given unto me in heaven and in earth* (Matthew 28:18), and *[I] have the keys of hell and of death* (Revelation 1:18).

> Jesus Christ, by His death and resurrection, was granted by the Father to be Lord and head over all things.

All things, then, whether visible or invisible, *whether they be thrones, or dominions, or principalities, or powers; all things were created by him, and for him* (Colossians 1:16). Because of this, *at the name of Jesus every knee should bow, . . . and that every tongue should confess that Jesus Christ is Lord, to the glory of God the Father* (Philippians 2:10-11). In order that this may be done, He has His verdict upon a judgment day, in which He, to show Himself His people, His way, and His Word in their glory, will have all His enemies raised out of their graves and brought before Him, where He will sit over them in the throne of His glory and will then show them *who is the blessed and only Potentate, the King of kings, and Lord of lords* (1 Timothy 6:14-15; see also Matthew 25:31-32).

Behold, He comes *with ten thousands of his saints, to execute judgment upon all, and to convince all that are ungodly among them of all their ungodly deeds which they have ungodly committed, and of all their hard speeches which ungodly sinners have spoken against him* (Jude 1:14-15).

Fifth, the great preparation that God has made for the judgment of the wicked clearly demonstrates their rising forth out of their graves:

1. He has appointed the day of their rising.

2. He has appointed their judge to judge them.

3. He has recorded all their words and actions against that day.

4. He has also already appointed the witnesses to come in against them.

5. The instruments of death and misery are already prepared for them.

   a. He has appointed the day of their rising. John calls this day *the time of the dead, that they should be judged* (Revelation 11:18). Paul says this is a fixed time: *He hath appointed a day in which he will judge the world* (Acts 17:31). Christ narrows this specific time and day down to an hour, saying, *The hour is coming, in* the which all that are in the graves shall hear his voice, and shall come forth (John 5:28-29).

b.   As He has appointed the day, so He has appointed the judge: *He hath appointed a day, in the which he will judge the world in righteousness by that man whom he hath ordained; whereof he hath given assurance to all men, in that he hath raised him from the dead* (Acts 17:31). This man is Jesus Christ; for it is He who is *ordained of God to be the Judge of quick and dead* (Acts 10:42).

c.   All their deeds and works, to a word and thought, are each already recorded and enrolled in the books of the laws of heaven against that day. *The sin of Judah is written with a pen of iron, and with the point of a diamond: it is graven upon the table of their heart* (Jeremiah 17:1). God said, *Write it before them in a table, and note it in a book, that it may be for the time to come, even for ever and ever, that this is a rebellious people* (Isaiah 30:8-9).

d.   God has prepared His witnesses against this day (James 5:1-3; Job 20:27; Matthew 24:14; Romans 2:14-15; Malachi 3:5).

e.   The instruments of death and eternal misery are already prepared. *He hath also prepared for him the instruments of death; he ordaineth his arrows against the persecutors* (Psalm 7:13). Hell has been prepared long ago. *He hath made it deep and large* (Isaiah 30:33). The fire, the everlasting fire, has also been prepared long ago (Matthew 25:41). The heavy weights of God's curses are also ready (Deuteronomy 29:20), and their *judgment now of a long time lingereth not, and their damnation slumbereth not* (2 Peter 2:3).

How ridiculous a business would all this be if these things would all be prepared by the only wise God, and there would be none to be judged; or if He who is ordained judge should not, either through lack of power or will, command these rebels and force them before His judgment seat! The sinners would indeed be glad if these things might be true. They would be glad in their very hearts if they could be in their secret places of darkness and in the grave forever, but it must not be. The day of their rising is set. The judge is appointed. Their deeds are written. The deep dungeon is ever waiting for them with open mouth. At the day appointed, neither earth nor death nor hell can hinder. *There shall be a resurrection of the dead, both of the just and unjust.*

> The sinners would be glad in their hearts if they could be in their secret places of darkness forever, but it must not be. The day of their rising is set.

Sixth and lastly, besides what has already been said, I believe there will be a resurrection of the wicked at the last day because of the ungodly consequences and errors that most naturally follow the denial thereof, as explained below.

1. He who takes away the doctrine of the resurrection of the wicked takes away one of the main arguments that God has provided to convince a sinner of the evil of his ways. How will a sinner be convinced of the evil of sin if he is not convinced of the certainty of eternal judgment? How will he be convinced of eternal judgment if you convince him that when he is dead, he will not at all rise – especially since the resurrection of the dead must unavoidably be the forerunner of eternal judgment (Hebrews 6:2)? It was Paul's reasoning of *righteousness, temperance, and judgment to come* that made Felix tremble (Acts 24:25). It is this also that he called the argument of terror by which

he persuaded people (2 Corinthians 5:10-11). This was Solomon's argument (Ecclesiastes 11:9), and this was also Christ's argument, where He said *that every idle word that men shall speak, they shall give account thereof in the day of judgment* (Matthew 12:36).

2. Those who deny the resurrection of the wicked both acknowledge and maintain the main doctrine of the Ranters, along with most of the corrupt people in the world. The Ranters deny it both in principle and practice, and the others deny it in practice at least. It is very strange to me that these people above all others would both know and live in the doctrines of the kingdom of God, especially since the denial of this doctrine is an evident sign of someone who is appointed to wrath and destruction (2 Timothy 2:18).[3]

To be clear, however, *there shall be a resurrection of the dead, both of the just and unjust.* Therefore, no matter what others may say or profess, being deceived by Satan and their own hearts, yet fear Him who can *destroy both soul and body in hell* (Matthew 10:28).

There shall be a resurrection of the dead, both of the just and unjust (Acts 24:15). *And the sea gave up the dead which were in it; and death and hell delivered up the dead which were in them* (Revelation 20:13).

---

3   Unsanctified knowledge, accompanied by a degree of conformity in conduct, may be the portion of some who indulge soul-destroying heresies (George Offor, Editor).

The Manner of the Resurrection of the Wicked

Having shown you that the wicked must arise, I will now show you the manner of their rising. Notice that just as the very title of the just and unjust are opposites, so they are in all other matters, as well as in their resurrections.

First then, while the just in their resurrection come forth in incorruption, the unjust in their resurrection will come forth in their corruptions. For although the ungodly at their resurrection will forever after be incapable of having body and soul separate, or of their being annihilated into nothing, yet they will not rise in incorruption. If they were to arise in incorruption, they must arise to life, and also must have the conquest over sin and death (1 Corinthians 15:55), but that they will not have. It is the righteous only, who put on incorruption, who are swallowed up by life.

The wicked's resurrection is called *the resurrection of damnation* (John 5:29). In their very resurrection, these people will be hurt by the second death. They will arise in death, and will be under it, under the pains and terrors of it, the entire time of their arraignment. A living death, as it were, will feed upon them. They will never be spiritually alive, nor yet completely dead. Rather, their experience will be much like that of one upon whom natural death and hell, by reason of the person's guilt, feeds on him who is going before the judge to receive his condemnation to the gallows.

Even though a felon leaves prison when he is going to stand before the judge for his trial, yet he is not out of prison, or even free from his chains, which are still making a noise on his heels, and the thoughts of what he is to soon hear from the judge is still terrifying and afflicting his heart. Death, like some evil spirit or ghost, continually haunts him and plays the butcher continually in his soul and conscience, with visions and fears about the thoughts of the sudden and insupportable consequences he will soon meet with.

The wicked will come out of their graves still having the chains of eternal death hanging on them and having the claws of that dreadful ghost fastened in their souls. Life will be as far from them as heaven is from hell. This morning to them is even as the shadow of death. They will then be in the very *terrors of the shadow of death* (Job 24:17). As Christ said, *Their worm dieth not, and the fire is not quenched* (Mark 9:44). From death to eternity, it will never be quenched. Their bed is now among the flames, and when they rise, they will rise in flames. While they stand before the Judge, they will stand in flames, even in the flames of a guilty conscience. As they come before the Judge, they will be within the very jaws of death and destruction.

The ungodly will be far from rising as the saints, for they will be even in the region and shadow of death. The first moment of their rising, death will be ever over them, ever feeding on their souls, ever presenting to their hearts the heights and depths of the misery that now must seize them and, like a bottomless gulf, must swallow them up. *They shall move out of their holes like worms of the earth: they shall be afraid of the* LORD *our God* (Micah 7:17).

Second, while the resurrection of the godly will be a resurrection in glory, the resurrection of the wicked will be a resurrection in dishonor. Yes, as the glory of saints, at the day of their rising, will be glory unspeakable, so the dishonor of the ungodly at that day will be dishonor beyond expression. As Daniel said, the good will rise to everlasting life, but the wicked will rise *to shame and everlasting contempt* (Daniel 12:2).

The psalmist wrote, *O Lord, when thou awakest* (that is, to judge them), *thou shalt despise their image* (Psalm 73:20). Never was toad or serpent more loathsome to anyone than these souls will be in the eyes of God in their rising forth from their graves. Job said that when they go to their graves, *his bones are full of the sin of his youth, which shall lie down with him in the dust* (Job 20:11). They will arise in the same offensive and stinking condition, for as death leaves, so judgment finds them. At the resurrection of these ungodly, they will be in a very loathsome condition.

> The ungodly at their death are like the thistle seed, but at their rising, they will be like the thistle that is grown; they will be more repulsive and offensive.

The ungodly at their death are like the thistle seed, but at their rising, they will be like the thistle that is grown; they will be more repulsive and offensive and will provoke abundant rejection.

Such dishonor, shame, and contempt will appear in them that neither God nor Christ, saints nor angels, will so much as once regard them or allow them once to come near them. He beholds the wicked *afar off* (Psalm 138:6) because in the day of grace, they would not come to Him and be saved, so therefore now they will, all as thorns, be *thrust away* as with fences of iron (2 Samuel 23:6-7). Their rising is called the resurrection of the unjust, and they will appear as the unjust at that day. They will more stink in the nostrils of God, and in the nostrils of all the heavenly hosts, more than if they had the most bothersome plague sores in the world oozing on them.

If a man at his birth is considered as one cast forth to the loathing of his person (Ezekiel 16:5), then how loathsome, offensive, dishonorable, and contemptible will those be who will arise without God, without Christ, without the Holy Spirit, and without grace when the trumpet sounds for their judgment! They will come out of their graves far more loathsome and filthy than if they would ascend out of the most filthy hole on earth.

Third, while the just will arise in power, the wicked and unjust will rise in weakness and fear. Sin and guilt bring weakness and instability in this life; how much more when sin and guilt, with all their power and force, like a giant, fasten on them! As God says, *Can thine heart endure, or can thine hands be strong, in the days that I shall deal with thee?* (Ezekiel 22:14). The dreadful jaws of despair will then glare at you. Conscience, like thunderclaps, will continually condemn you and batter against your weary spirit.

The godly will have *boldness in the day of judgment* (1 John 4:17), but the wicked will be like *the chaff which the wind driveth away* (Psalm 1:4). Oh, the fear and the heartache that will seize them in their rising! Oh, the frightful thoughts that then will fill their throbbing hearts! That soul that has been in hellfire among the demons must possess the body again. It will possess it with the hot scalding stench of hell upon it.

They will not be able to lift up their heads forever. *Therefore shall all hands be faint, and every man's heart shall melt: and they shall be afraid: pangs and sorrows shall take hold of them; they shall be in pain as a woman that travaileth: they shall be amazed one at another; their faces shall be as flames* (Isaiah 13:7-8). Everything they see, hear, or think of will lead to their discomfort. Those whom God has left, whom guilt has seized, and whom death is swallowing up forever must necessarily be weak.

Fourth, while the just shall arise as spiritual bodies, the unjust will arise only as mere helpless lumps of sinful nature, not having the least help from God to bear them up under this condition. Wherefore, as soon as they are risen out of their graves, they will feel a continual sinking under every remembrance of every sin and thought of judgment. In their rising, they fall; they fall from that moment and forever.

This is why the dungeon into which they fall is called *bottomless* (Revelation 20:1). Just as there will be no end of their misery, so there will be no stay or support to bear them up in it. As I said before, they will not now, as before, be separate body from soul, but both together will be bound in the cords of sin and iniquity, in which they will then tremble as thieves, murderers, etc., as they go before the Judge to hear what He will say unto them.

When the wicked are raised out of their graves, they will, together with all the angels of darkness (their fellow prisoners), be brought up, being shackled in their sins, to the place of judgment. Sitting in judgment will be Jesus Christ, the King of kings and Lord of lords, the Lord Chief Judge of things in heaven, and things in earth, and things under the earth. On His right hand and left will sit all the princes and heavenly nobles, the saints and prophets, and the apostles and witnesses of Jesus – each one in his kingly attire upon the throne of his glory (Joel 3:11-14). Then will be fulfilled that which is written, *But those mine enemies, which would not that I should reign over them, bring hither, and slay them* (Luke 19:27).

The Judgment of the Wicked

When everyone is set in his proper place, when the Judge is on His throne, with His attendants around Him and with the prisoners coming up for judgment – then there will directly issue forth a mighty fire and tempest from before the throne that will compass it round about. The fire will be as bars and boundaries to the wicked to keep them at a certain distance from the heavenly Majesty. As David said, *Our God shall come, and shall not keep silence; a fire shall devour before him, and it shall be very tempestuous round about him* (Psalm 50:3). Daniel wrote, *His throne was like the fiery flame, and his wheels as burning fire. A fiery stream issued and came forth from before him* (Daniel 7:9-10).

With this preparation being made – the Judge on the throne with His attendants near Him; the judgment seat for the prisoners, and the rebels all standing with fearful faces to look at what comes next, then presently the books are brought out – the books both of death and life, and every one of them is opened before the sinners, who are now to be judged and condemned. For after Daniel said, *A fiery stream issued and came forth from before him*, he added, *Thousand thousands ministered unto him, and ten thousand times ten thousand stood before him:*

the judgment was set, and the books were opened (Daniel 7:10). The apostle John added:

> *I saw a great white throne, and him that sat on it,*
> *from whose face the earth and the heaven fled away;*
> *and there was found no place for them. And I saw*
> *the dead, small and great, stand before God; and the*
> *books were opened: and another book was opened,*
> *which is the book of life: and the dead were judged*
> *out of those things which were written in the books,*
> *according to their works.* (Revelation 20:11-12)

He did not say that the book was opened, as of one, but *the books*, as of many. Indeed, there are more than one, two, or three books out of which the dead in the judgment will be judged.

  a. First, there is the book of the creatures to be opened.

  b. Second, there is the book of God's remembrance.

  c. Third, there is the book of the law.

  d. Fourth, there is the book of life.

By every one of these, that is, out of what is written in them, the world of the ungodly will be judged.

And the books were opened.

The Book of the Creatures

First, the book of the creatures will be opened. It is opened first because it concerns man's nature and also it relates to all other creatures.

1. He will show in what the principles of nature were, as they were God's creation, and how the world has walked, acted, and done contrary to these principles.

The principles of nature are arranged under three general points.

   1. That man, by his own natural reason and judgment, may conclude that there is a God, a deity, a main, first, or principal Being who is over all and is supreme above all. Man finds this sentiment in himself simply because he is a rational creature. This is why all heathens who mind their own natural reason conclude that we are His offspring; that is, that we are His creation and workman-ship; that He made heaven and earth, and *hath made of one blood all nations of men*; and that *in him we live, and move, and have our being* (Acts 17:24-29).

      a. It appears further that man by his own nature knows that there is such a God by his being able to judge by nature that there is such a thing as sin. As Christ said, *Why even of yourselves judge ye not what is right?* (Luke 12:57). It is as if He had said, "You are degenerated even from the principles of nature and right reason." As Paul said in another place, *Doth not even nature itself teach you?* (1 Corinthians 11:14). Now if he can judge that there is such a thing as sin, it must necessarily be that he understands that there is a God to whom sin is opposite; for if there is no God, there is no sin against Him, and he who does not know the one does not know the other.

b. It is further evident that man by nature knows that there is a God by those fits of fear and dread that are often begotten in themselves, even in every person who breathes in this world; for they are convicted and reproved, judged and condemned, by their own consciences and thoughts, even though they know neither Moses nor Christ. *For when the Gentiles, which have not the law, do by nature the things contained in the law, these, having not the law, are a law unto themselves: which shew the work of the law written in their hearts* (Romans 2:14-15). That is, by this very thing they hold forth to all men – that God created them in that state and quality so that they might in and by their own nature judge and know that there is a God – they demonstrate that they know there is a God.

It further shows itself, Paul said, by those workings of heart, convictions of conscience, and accusations that every thought makes within them, together with the fear that is begotten in them, when they transgress or do those things that are irrational or contrary to what they see they will do. I might add further that the natural tendency that is in all people to devotion and religion, of one kind or another, clearly tells us that they, by the book of nature (which book is themselves), read that there is one great and eternal God.

2. The second principle of nature is that this God should be sought after by man so that they might enjoy communion with Him forever. As I said before, the light of nature shows man that there is a great God, even God who made the world. The purpose of its showing him this is *that they should seek the Lord, if haply they might feel after him, and find him, though he be not far from every one of us* (Acts 17:27).

> The light of nature shows man that there is a great God.

3. This light of nature teaches that men should do that which is just and equal between themselves. As Moses said long before the law was given, *Sirs, ye are brethren; why do ye wrong one another?* (Acts 7:26; Exodus 2:13). It is as if he said, "You are of equal creation. You are the same flesh. You both judge that it is not equally done of any to do you wrong, and therefore you should judge by the same reason so that you should not wrong one another."

Every person in the whole world has transgressed against every one of these three principles. As Paul said, *Both Jews and Gentiles . . . are all under sin* (Romans 3:9).

a. In regard to the Jews, who is he who has honored, reverenced, worshipped, and adored the living God to the height both of what they saw in Him and also according to the goodness and mercy they have as men received from Him? All have *worshipped and served the creature more than the Creator, who is blessed for ever* (Romans 1:25), and so have walked contrary to, and have sinned against, this bond of nature in this first principle.

b. Instead of minding their own future happiness as nature teaches, people have, through giving way to sin and Satan, minded nothing less; for although reason teaches all people to love that which is good and profitable, yet they, contrary to this, have loved that which is hurtful and destructive. Yes, even though sense teaches to avoid the danger that is apparent, yet man, contrary to both reason and sense, even all people, have rejected their own happiness both against light and feeling. As Paul said, *Who knowing the judgment of God, that they which commit such things are worthy of death, not only do the same, but have pleasure in them that do them* (Romans 1:32).

c. Instead of doing what is fair and right, and as he would want to be treated, which nature itself teaches, he has given himself up to vile affections, *being filled*, by refusing the dictates of nature, *with all unrighteousness, fornication, wickedness, covetousness, maliciousness; full of envy, murder, debate, deceit, malignity; whisperers, backbiters, haters of God, despiteful, proud, boasters, inventors of evil things, disobedient to parents, without understanding, covenant breakers, without natural affection, implacable, unmerciful* (Romans 1:29-31).

Notice that he does not say that all these things are put into practice by every person, but that every person has all these in his heart, which there defile the soul and make it abominable in the sight of God. They are filled with all unrighteousness, which also appears, as occasion serves, sometimes one of them, sometimes more. Man, having sinned against that natural light, judgment, reason, and conscience that God has given him, therefore, though, as I said before, he knew neither Moses nor

Christ, yet he will perish. Paul said, *As many as have sinned without law shall also perish without law* (Romans 2:12).

Yes, man will be found here not only to be a sinner against God, but to be an opposer of himself, a contradictor of his own nature, and one who will not do that which he judges even of himself to be right (2 Timothy 2:25). Their sin is written upon the tables of their own heart (Jeremiah 17:1), and their own wickedness and backsliding will both correct and reprove them (Jeremiah 2:19).

If we consider how unique a creature man was made by God, it is astonishing to behold how much below, besides, and against that state and place man acts and does in this state of sin and degeneracy. Man in his creation was made in the image of God (Genesis 1:26), but man, by reason of his yielding to the Tempter, has made himself the very figure and image of the devil. Man by creation was made upright and sinless, but man by sin has made himself crooked and sinful (Ecclesiastes 7:29). Man by creation had all the powers of his soul at liberty to study God, his creator, and His glorious attributes and being, but man by sin has so bound up his own senses and reason, and has given way for blindness and ignorance of God to reign in his soul, that he is now captivated and held bound in alienation and separation both from God and from all things truly spiritually good. Paul wrote that the reason for this is because *when they knew God, they glorified him not as God, neither were thankful; but became vain in their imaginations, and their foolish heart was darkened* (Romans 1:21). Again Paul wrote, *Having the understanding darkened, being alienated from the life of God through the ignorance that is in them, because of the blindness of their heart* (Ephesians 4:18).

Man will be brought forth to the judgment for this abuse of the

> Man by creation was made upright and sinless, but man by sin has made himself crooked and sinful.

workmanship of God. He will be caught, convicted, and condemned as a rebel against both God and his own soul, as Paul affirms, and that was when he reasoned simply as a man (Romans 3:5-6).

When this part of the book regarding man's nature is opened, and man is convicted and condemned by it by reason of his sinning against the three general principles thereof, then the second part of the book will be opened.

2. Immediately after is the second part of the book opened, which is the mystery of the creatures.

The whole creation that is before you was not only made to show the power of God in themselves, but was also made to teach you and to preach to you, both much of God and yourself, as also the righteousness, and justice of God against sin.

> *For the wrath of God is revealed from heaven against*
> *all ungodliness and unrighteousness of men, who*
> *hold the truth in unrighteousness; because that*
> *which may be known of God is manifest in them;*
> *for God hath shewed it unto them. For the invis-*
> *ible things of him from the creation of the world are*
> *clearly seen, being understood by the things that are*
> *made, even his eternal power and Godhead; so that*
> *they are without excuse.* (Romans 1:18-20)

1. The creation of the world, then, of the heavens, earth, sun, moon, stars, with all other the creatures of God, preaches aloud to all people the eternal power and godhead of their Creator (Psalm 8:3). In wisdom He has made them all (Psalm 104:24). He made them to teach us. His creation carries instruction. He who is wise and will understand these things will understand the loving-kindness of the Lord, for *the works of the* LORD *are great, sought out of*

all them that have pleasure therein (Psalm 111:2; see also Psalm 107).

2. As the creation in general preaches to everyone something of God, so, too, it proclaims how man should behave himself both to God and to one another. In the judgment, God's creation will certainly testify against all those who will be found to have opposed and resisted what God by His creation proclaims to us.

   a. God's creation is obedient both to God and to man. To God, they are all in subjection (if you do not consider demons and humans). Even the very *dragons, and all deeps, fire, and hail; snow, and vapours* obey His word (Psalm 148:7-8). The winds and seas obey Him (Mark 4:41). By their obedience to God, they teach you obedience, and by their obedience, your disobedience will be condemned in the judgment (Psalm 147:15-18).

      Their obedience to you also teaches you obedience to all who are above you, *for every kind of beasts, and of birds, and of serpents, and of things in the sea, is tamed, and hath been tamed* and brought into obedience by mankind. Man only remains untamed and unruly, and therefore by these is condemned (James 3:7-8).

   b. The fruitfulness of all the creatures in their kind teaches and admonishes you to live a fruitful life toward God and in the things of His Holy Word. In the beginning, God said to let the earth bring forth fruit, grass, herbs, trees, beasts, creeping things, and cattle after their kind, and it was so (Genesis 1:11, 24). But to man, He has sent His prophets, *rising early and sending them, saying, Oh, do not this abominable thing that I hate* (Jeremiah 44:4), but they will not obey. For if the gentiles, who do not have the law, do by some acts of obedience condemn the wickedness of those who break the law by the letter and circumcision (Romans 2:14), how much more will the fruitfulness of all the creatures testify in the judgment against the whole world! As Job said, by the obedience and fruitfulness of the creatures, God judges, and so will judge, the people (Job 36:27-32).

c. The knowledge and wisdom of the creatures, upon examination, teach you wisdom and command you to be wise. The stork in the heaven, the swallow and the crane, by observing the time and season of their coming, admonish you to learn the time of grace and of the mercy of God (Jeremiah 8:7). The ox and the donkey, by the knowledge they have of their master's care, admonish you to know the bread and table of God, and both do and will condemn your ignorance of the food of heaven (Isaiah 1:3).

d. The labor and toil of the creatures convict you of sloth and idleness. *Go to the ant, thou sluggard; consider her ways, and be wise*, for the ant provides its food in the summer, and stores up food for difficult times (Proverbs 6:6-8). However, you spend the whole summer of your life in wasting both time and soul. *All things are full of labour*, Solomon said (Ecclesiastes 1:8). Only man spends *all the day idle* (Matthew 20:6), and his years are *as a tale that is told* (Psalm 90:9). The rock badgers are not mighty, yet they work hard to make a house in the rock to be safe from the rage of the hunter (Proverbs 30:26).

The spider taketh hold with her hands, and is in kings' palaces (Proverbs 30:28). Only man turns himself upon the bed of sloth *as the door turns upon his hinges* (Proverbs 26:14). It is only mankind that will not lay hold on the Rock (Christ), as the rock badger teaches, nor lay hold on the kingdom of heaven, as the spider urges him to do (John 5:40).

e. The fear that is in all creatures when they perceive that danger is near teaches people to flee from the wrath to come. *In vain the net is spread in the sight of any bird* (Proverbs 1:17), but man only is the foolhardy creature that lies in wait for his own blood and sets an ambush for his own life (Proverbs 1:18). Every creature will fly, run, strive, and struggle to escape the danger it is sensible of; it is only man that delights to dance around the mouth of hell and to be knowingly captured in Satan's snare (Romans 1:32).

f. The dependence that all the creatures have upon God teaches you to depend on Him who made you, and who will in the judgment condemn you for your unlawful practices and faithless efforts for your preservation. The young ravens seek their food from God (Job 38:41; Psalm 147:9), and they will condemn your lying, cheating, overreaching, defrauding, and similar sinful practices to get ahead. The ravens provide neither storehouse nor barn (Luke 12:24), but you are so greedy of these things that for these things you shut yourself out of the kingdom of heaven!

> The dependence that all the creatures have upon God teaches you to depend on Him who made you.

g. The love and compassion that is in their hearts to their young and to one another will judge and condemn to your own soul the hard-heartedness that is in you.

What shall I say? *The heaven shall reveal his iniquity; and the earth shall rise up against him* (Job 20:27). That is, all the creatures of God, by their fruitfulness and subjection to the will of their Creator, will judge and condemn you for your disobedience and rebellion against Him.

3. As these creatures call unto you every day and lay these things before you, so God has creatures of another nature for your awakening in case you are asleep and senseless:

   a. Your bed, when you lie down in it, preaches to you your grave, your sleep, and your death. Your rising in the morning preaches to you your resurrection to judgment (Job 14:12; 17:13; Isaiah 26:19).

   b. The jail that you see with your eyes and the felons who look out through the bars of their cells put you in mind of the prison of hell and of the dreadful state of those who are there (Luke 12:58-59).

   c. The fire that burns in your fireplace proclaims the fire of hell unto you (Isaiah 10:16; Revelation 20:14).

   d. The unpleasant smell, stench, and steam of the burning brimstone shows you the loathsome, odious, and dreadful torments of hell (Revelation 19:20).

   e. The darkness of the night in solitary places, and the fears that commonly torment those who walk therein, preach to you the fears and dread, the terrors and dismay, that will forever attend all damned souls (Deuteronomy 28:65-67; Matthew 8:12).

   f. By delighting to lay sticks on the fire to warm yourself when you are cold, not caring how fiercely they burn therein as long as you can be warmed and refreshed

thereby, God preaches to you with what contented-
ness He will burn sinners in the flames of hell for the
easing of His mind and the satisfaction of His justice.
He says, *Ah, I will ease me of mine adversaries, and
avenge me of mine enemies* (Isaiah 1:24).

4. Yes, by blowing on the fire so that it may better burn the
   wood, you preach to yourself how God will blow the fire
   of hell by the strictness of His law so that by its flames it
   may, according to its purpose, kindle upon condemned
   sinners (Isaiah 30:33).

As inconsiderable and unlikely as these things may appear
to you now, in the judgment they will be found the items and
warning words of God to your souls. Know that He who could
overthrow the land of Egypt with frogs, lice, flies, locusts, etc.
will overthrow the world at the last day by the book of the
creatures, and that by the least and most careless of them, as
well as by the rest.

This book of the creatures is so excellent and so full, so easy
and so suiting the capacity of all, that there is not one person in
the world who is not is caught, convicted, and condemned by it.
This is the book that he who does not even know the alphabet
may read, and that he who saw neither Old or New Testament
may by it know much of both God and himself.

It is this book out of which generally both Job and his friends
did so profoundly converse about the judgments of God, and out
of which God Himself did so convincingly answer Job. Job was
as accomplished in this book as many of us are in the Scriptures,
and he could see further by it than many nowadays see by the
Old and New Testaments. This is the book out of which Christ,
the prophets, and the apostles so frequently speak by their
similitudes, proverbs, and parables as being the most easy way
to convince the world – although by reason of their ignorance,

nothing will work with them except what is set on their hearts by the Holy Spirit.

One more thing, and I will be done with this, and that is that God has sealed the judgment of the world by the book of the creatures – even by man's own stance unto such of them, which, through any impediment, have disappointed his expectations. For example, if you have a tree in your orchard that neither bears fruit nor is good for anything else, you are in favor of cutting it down and using it as fuel for the fire.

By making such a judgment, you do not much consider that you are passing judgment upon your own fruitless soul, but it is so: *And now also the axe is laid unto the root of the trees: therefore every tree which bringeth not forth good fruit is hewn down, and cast into the fire* (Matthew 3:10). For as truly as you say of your fruitless tree, "Cut it down. Why does it burden the ground?" so truly does your voice cause heaven to echo again upon your head, "Cut him down. Why does he burden the ground?" (Ezekiel 15:1-6; Luke 13:6-8).

Further, the tendency of your heart toward fruitless and unprofitable creatures preaches to you what the inclination of the heart of God toward you will be in the judgment. If you have a cow or any other beast that is now unprofitable to you, even if you may allow it to remain with you for a little while, as God allows sinners to remain in the world, yet all this while your heart is not with them, but you will take time to rid your hands of them. This is how it will be in the judgment. As God said, *Though Moses and Samuel stood before me* (that is, to ask me to spare this people), *yet my mind could not be toward this people: cast them out of my sight, and let them go forth* (Jeremiah 15:1; see also Ezekiel 14:13-14).

> If you have a cow that is now unprofitable, you may allow it to remain with you for a little while, as God allows sinners to remain in the world, but your heart is not with it.

This is how God will judge the world at the last day. He will declare to them how they have degenerated and gone back from the principles of nature in which He created them. He will show them how they have disregarded all the instructions that He had given them, even by the obedience, fruitfulness, wisdom, labor, fear, and love of the creatures. He will tell them in regard to their judgment that they themselves have decided it, both by cutting down that which was fruitless, and by withdrawing their hearts from those things that to them were unprofitable. *As therefore the tares are gathered and burned in the fire, so shall it be in the end of the world* (Matthew 13:40). As men deal with weeds and rotten wood, so will God deal with sinners in the day of judgment. He will bring in all the counsels and warnings He has given people by these things, both to clear up and to intensify their judgment to them.

The Book of God's Remembrance

The second book that will be opened at this day is the book of God's remembrance (Malachi 3:16). For as God has in His remembrance recorded all and every specific good thing that His own people have done to and for His name while they were in this world, so He has in His remembrance recorded all the evil and sin of His adversaries – everything (Ecclesiastes 12:14).

God's remembrance is so perfect in every way that it is impossible that anything should be lost that is committed to it to be kept, and it will all be brought forth to the judgment at the appointed time. For as a thousand years are but as yesterday with His eternity, so the sins that have been committed thousands of years ago are all so firmly fixed in the remembrance of the eternal God that they are always as fresh and clear in His sight as if they were only just now being committed.

He calls up again the things that are past (Ecclesiastes 3:15), and He has set *our [most] secret sins in the light of [His] countenance* (Psalm 90:8). As the Bible says in another place, *Hell [itself] is naked before him, and destruction hath no covering* (Job 26:6). That is, the most secret, scheming, wicked, and hidden contrivances of the most devious of the infernal spirits, which yet are far more shrewd than men, will not be able to be hidden from God. Yet all their ways, hearts, and most secret words, thoughts, and deeds are completely clear in the eyes of the great God. All things are open and bare before *the eyes of him with whom we have to do* (Hebrews 4:13). He *will bring to light the hidden things of darkness, and will make manifest the counsels of the hearts* (1 Corinthians 4:5).

Yet they say, *The* LORD *shall not see, neither shall the God of Jacob regard it. Understand, ye brutish among the people: and ye fools, when will ye be wise? He that planted the ear, shall he not hear? He that formed the eye, shall he not see? He that chastiseth the heathen, shall not he correct? He that teacheth man knowledge, shall not he know?* (Psalm 94:7-10; see also Hosea 7:2; 8:13). *Can any hide himself in secret places that I shall not see him?* (that is, when he is committing wickedness) *saith the* LORD: *Do not I fill heaven and earth? saith the* LORD (Jeremiah 23:24).

To know and see things is the reason among people why they remember. Wherefore, to show us that He will remember all our sins if we die out of Christ, God tells us that He knows and sees them all, and therefore must necessarily remember them; for as His sight and knowledge are, so is His remembrance of all things.

> When this book of Gods remembrance is opened in the judgment then will be brought forth whatsoever has been done since the world began.

Therefore, when this book of His remembrance is opened in the judgment, as it will be, then will be brought forth from their hidden holes all things, whatsoever has been done since the world began, whether by kingdoms in general or by individuals in particular. Then also will be brought out into open view all the transactions of God and His Son among the sons of men, and everything will be applied to every individual person, in equity and justice, to whom they belong. The sins that you have committed will be your own, and you yourself will bear them. *The LORD is a God of knowledge, and by him actions are weighed* (1 Samuel 2:3).

It will be marvelous to behold how by thousands, and ten thousands, God will call from their secret places those sins that one would have thought had been dead and buried and forgotten. Yes, He will show before the sun such things that are so evil and so horrid that one would think it was not in the hearts of any to commit; for all is recorded in the book of God's remembrance.

While people are here on earth, they have a thousand tricks to present themselves to others as being far more fair and honest than they are, or ever were. As Christ said to the Pharisees, *Ye are they which justify yourselves before men; but God knoweth your hearts* (Luke 16:15). God indeed knows what a nest, what an abundance, what swarms, yes, what legions of hellish wickednesses there are lurking with power, like cockatrices,[4] in those people who one would swear a thousand times are good and honest people. The way of men in their sins is like *an eagle in the air; the way of a serpent upon a rock; the way of a ship in the midst of the sea; and the way of a man with a maid,* Solomon said (Proverbs 30:19). That is, secretly and carefully, attempting to justify and excuse their sinful deeds and thoughts, they wipe their mouths at the end of their evil and say, *I have done no wickedness* (Proverbs 30:20).

Although this may serve for the time present, and no longer, God will not be deceived, blinded, or mocked (Galatians 6:7). He will accept no excuses. *They consider not in their hearts that I remember all their wickedness,* God says (Hosea 7:2), *but I will reprove thee, and set them in order before thine eyes* (Psalm 50:21).

The very heart of Cain the murderer will be laid open here, as well as the hearts of Judas the traitor, Saul the adversary

---

4   A cockatrice is a serpent that, according to legend, hatched from the egg of a
     rooster and has a deadly glance.

of David, and of those that under pretenses of holiness have persecuted Christ, His Word, and His people. Then will every drunkard, fornicator, thief, and every other wicked person be turned inside out. Their hearts will be opened, and every sin, with every circumstance of place, time, person involved, and the causes that drew them to the commission of every evil will be revealed to all. There will be no hiding yourselves behind curtains or covering yourselves with the black and dark night. *If I say, Surely the darkness shall cover me; even the night shall be light about me: Yea, [O God], the darkness hideth not from thee; but the night shineth as the day: the darkness and the light are both alike to thee* (Psalm 139:11-12).

The piercing eye of God beholds all places, people, and things. The holy hand of His justice writes them down in the book of His remembrance. By His power and wisdom, He will open and read to all people exactly, distinctly, and convincingly whatever has been said or thought by them or has been done by them in their whole life. *For all these things God will bring thee into judgment* (Ecclesiastes 11:9). Again, as God will show from the book of His remembrance whatever has been done, thought, or said by you against Him, so also will He then bring forth by the same book all things and conduct of His toward you.

He will bring to your mind every sermon that you have heard, every chapter you have read, every conviction you have had on your conscience, and every admonition that has been given to you in all your life when you were in the land of the living.

God will then lay open before you the patience He extended to you, how He let you live one year, two years, ten years, even twenty and thirty and forty years, and all to test you. Yes, He will now also bring to your view how many times He warned, rebuked, threatened, and corrected you for your wickedness. He will show you how many awakening providences and judgments He continually laid before your face, how many times you, like

Balaam, ran upon the point of the sword of justice, and how He drew back, as being unwilling to kill you (Numbers 22:23-34).

Also brought before you and all people will be how many struggles God had with your heart in your difficulties and illnesses to do good to you, and at such times, how many vows, promises, engagements, and resolutions you made before God to change and turn to Him if He would release you from your affliction and take off His rod from your back. Yet like the man possessed (Mark 5:1-5), you broke and snapped in two all these chains of iron with which you had bound your soul, and you did so simply for lust and sin.

Here also will be opened before you how often you have sinned against your light and knowledge, how often you have laid violent hands on your own conscience, and how often you have labored to put out that light that has stood in your way to hinder you from sinning against your soul. What a condition the Christless soul will be in at this day! How every one of these things will afflict the condemned soul! They will pierce like arrows, bite like serpents, and sting like adders.

With what shame will that person stand before the judgment seat of Christ who will have everything he has done against God, to provoke the eyes of His glory to jealousy, laid open before the whole host of the heavenly company! It would make a person ashamed to have his pockets searched for things that are stolen in the midst of a market, especially if he stands upon his reputation and honor. But you will have your heart, the very bottom of your heart, searched, and this will happen before your neighbor whom you have wronged, and before the demons whom you have served – yes, and before God, whom you have despised, and before the angels, those holy and delicate creatures whose holy and pure faces will hardly keep from blushing while God is making you vomit up all you have swallowed – for God will bring it out of your belly (Job 20:12-15).

Just as God forgetting iniquity is one of the main points of the covenant of grace, and is an argument of the highest nature to bring about and to continue consolation in the godly, so the remembrance of iniquity by the Lord is one of the heaviest loads and judgments that can happen to any poor creature.

That which the Lord forgets is forgiven forever, but that which He remembers is charged forever, and nothing can take it away.

Lord, remember not against us former iniquities (Psalm 79:8). *If thou, Lord, shouldst mark iniquities, O Lord, who shall stand?* (Psalm 130:3).

The reason is because that which the Lord forgets is forgiven forever (Romans 4:6-8; Hebrews 8:12), but that which He remembers is charged forever, and nothing can take it away. *Though thou wash thee with nitre, and take thee much soap, yet thine iniquity is marked before me, saith the Lord God* (Jeremiah 2:22).

The Book of the Law

The third book that will be opened on this day, and the book out of which God will judge the world, is the book of the law, or the Ten Commandments given forth on Mount Sinai. But this book will more specifically concern those who have received it, or who have had knowledge thereof. Everyone will not be judged by this book as having had it in their possession, but those who did not have knowledge of the Ten Commandments will be judged by the works of it, which are written in their hearts. *As many as have sinned without law shall also perish without law: and as many as have sinned in the law shall be judged by the law* (Romans 2:12). That is, the heathens who never knew the law as delivered on Sinai will be judged by the law as it was written in man's heart in his creation, which is comprised within the book of the creatures. However, those who have knowledge of the law as delivered on Sinai will be judged by the law as it was given there.

When this book is opened at the day of judgment, to those to whom it especially relates, it will be a most fearful law, far surpassing the two mentioned previously. This law is the primary and most pure resemblance of the justice and holiness of the heavenly majesty, and it proclaims to all people the sharpness and keenness of His wrath above the other two that I have before mentioned because it has been delivered more plainly and openly, both as to the duty required and the sin prohibited, and therefore must of necessity fall with more violence upon the heads of all who will be found within the compass of it. This law to be opened on this day contains two general points.

The first point is the revelation of the evil of sin, for it is so much against plain light and truth. The second point is the revelation of the vanity of all things that will on this day be brought by sinners for their help and plea at the judgment. Who cannot imagine that the poor world, at the day of their arraignment, would gather up all that they can ever think of as arguments to shelter them from the execution of that fierce wrath that then, with sinking souls, they will see prepared for them?

1. As to the first of these points, the apostle Paul told us that *the law entered, that the offence might abound* (Romans 5:20), or to reveal what it is. As he also said, *I had not known sin, but by the law* (Romans 7:7; see also Romans 7:13). So it is in this life, and so it will be in the day of judgment, that those who see sin, and who see it in its abounding nature and in its exceeding sinfulness, must see it by the law, for that is indeed the glass by which God reveals sin and the filthy spots of leprosy that are in the soul (James 1:22-25).

Those who do not have the happiness to see their sin by the law in this life, while there is a fountain of grace to wash in and to be made clean, must have the misery to see it at the judgment, when nothing is left but misery and pain as the punishment for the same. On that day, those little parts of this holy law that people now so easily overlook and sin against with ease will appear with such dread and with such fiery justice against every offense committed that if heaven and earth itself would step in to shelter the sinner from the justice and wrath due to sin, it would turn them up by the roots. *It is easier for heaven and earth to pass, than one tittle of the law to fail* (Luke 16:17). If there appeared such flames, thunderings, and tempests as there were when the law was given, imagine what flames and blackness will appear at the prosecution of that law! If there appeared so much holiness and justice at the giving of the law that it made all Israel tremble (Exodus 19:16) – yes, it made even holy Moses *exceedingly fear and quake* (Hebrews 12:21) – what will become of those whom God will judge by the rigor of this law in the day of judgment?

Oh, what thunderings and lightnings, what earthquakes and tempests, will there be in every condemned soul at the opening of this book! God will indeed visit them then *with thunder, and with earthquake, and great noise, with storm and tempest, and the flame of devouring fire* (Isaiah 29:6). *For behold*, the prophet Isaiah said, *the LORD will come with fire, and with his chariots like a whirlwind, to render his anger with fury, and his rebuke with flames of fire* (Isaiah 66:15).

The Lord will come with fire. That is, He will come in the flaming heat of His justice and holiness against sin and sinners to execute the firmness of His threatenings upon their perishing souls.

2. The second general point that is contained in this law that will be opened on this day is its exactness, purity, and strictness in regard to all acts of good that any poor creature has done in this life, whereby he in the judgment will desire to shelter or secure himself from the wrath of God. This is the rule and line and plumb line whereby every act of every person will be measured (Romans 3:21-22). He whose righteousness is not found adequate in every way to this law (which all

> He whose righteousness is not found adequate (which all will fall short of unless they have the righteousness of God by faith in Jesus Christ) must perish.

will fall short of unless they have the righteousness of God by faith in Jesus Christ) must perish. *Judgment also will I lay to the line, and righteousness to the plummet: and the hail shall sweep away the refuge of lies, and the waters shall overflow the hiding place* (Isaiah 28:17). That is, although people may not shelter themselves under legal repentance, cold profession, good meaning, intentions, and works, yet all these things must be measured and weighed in the balance of God's most righteous law. As I said already, whatever in that day is not found to be the righteousness of God will be found to be a refuge of lies and will be drowned by the overflowing of the wrath of God, as the waters of Noah overflowed the world.

This is the reason why all the ungodly will on that day be found as stubble, and the law as fire (Malachi 4:1). As the Scripture says, *From his right hand went a fiery law* (Deuteronomy 33:2), and *his lips are full of indignation, and his tongue as a devouring fire* (Isaiah 30:27). For as fire, which catches, burns, consumes, destroys, and devours, so the law will do to all those who on that day will be found under the transgression of the least part of it. It will be with these souls at the day of judgment as it is with those countries that are overrun by the most merciless conquerors, who do not leave anything behind them, but swallow up everything with fire and sword. *For by fire and by his sword will the LORD plead with all flesh: and the slain of the LORD shall be many* (Isaiah 66:16).

There are two things at the day of judgment that will meet in their height and utmost strength, and they are sin and the law, for the judgment will not be until the iniquity of the world is fully ripe (Joel 3:13; Revelation 14:15-20).

Now then, when sin is come to its full, having done all the harm it can do against the Lord of glory, then God brings forth the law, His holy and righteous law, and one of the two – either the law or sin – will now reign forever. Therefore, sin and sinners must tremble, along with all who help and support them – for God *will magnify the law, and make it honourable* (Isaiah 42:21). That is, God will give it the victory over the world forever, for it is holy, just, and good, while they are unholy, unjust, and bad. Therefore, by this law the Lord *shall rain snares, fire and brimstone, and an horrible tempest: this shall be the portion of their cup* (Psalm 11:6).

Let no one say, then, that because God is so well-known for His mercy and patience in this day of His grace, that therefore He will not be fierce and dreadful in His justice in the day of judgment. Judgment and justice are the last things that God intends to bring upon the stage, which will then be fully as fearful as now His goodness, patience, and long-suffering are admirable. Lord, *who knoweth the power of thine anger? Even according to thy fear, so is thy wrath* (Psalm 90:11).

If you wish, you may see a few of the sparks of the justice of God against sin and sinners, such as by His casting off angels for sin from heaven to hell; by His drowning the old world; and by His burning of Sodom and Gomorrah to ashes, condemning them *with an overthrow*, making them an example to those who after *should live ungodly* (2 Peter 2:4-6; Jude 1:6-7).

For *what things soever the law saith, it saith to them who are under the law; that every mouth may be stopped, and all the world may become guilty before God* (Romans 3:19).

Moses seems to be amazed that the children of Israel could continue to live after they only heard the law delivered on the mountain: *Did ever people hear the voice of God speaking out of the midst of the fire, as thou hast heard, and live?* (Deuteronomy 4:33). Oh, that you only knew the law, and the wondrous things that are written therein, before the Lord causes that fearful voice to be heard: *Cursed is every one that continueth not in all things that are written in the book of the law to do them* (Galatians 3:10). This curse must fall on all who do not walk in all the commandments of God without iniquity (Ezekiel 33:15). Of course, none can do this unless they walk in Christ, who alone has fulfilled all the commandments (Colossians 2:10).

The law is that which stands at the entrance of the paradise of God as a flaming sword, turning every way to keep out those who are not righteous with the righteousness of God (Genesis 3:24), and who do not have the readiness to come to the throne of grace by that *new and living way, which he hath consecrated for us through the veil; that is to say, his flesh* (Hebrews 10:20).

For although this law is taken away by Christ Jesus for all who truly and savingly believe (Colossians 2:14), yet it remains in full force and power, in every part of it, against every soul of man that will be found in his tabernacle – that is, in himself, and out of the Lord Jesus (Romans 3:19). It lies like a lion unrestrained at the gates of heaven, and will roar upon every unconverted soul, fiercely accusing every soul who would now gladly enter in through the gates into this city (Job 18:14; John 5:45).

So, then, he who can meet all of the law's most perfect and legal commands, and who can live in the midst of devouring fire and can there enjoy God and comfort himself, will dwell on high and will not be hurt by this law. *His place of defence shall be the munitions of rocks: bread shall be given him; his waters shall be sure. Thine eyes shall see the king in his beauty: they shall behold the land that is very far off* (Isaiah 33:16-17).

> He who can live in the midst of devouring fire and can there enjoy God and comfort himself, will dwell on high and will not be hurt by this law.

Blessed, then, is he whose righteousness meets every point of the law of God. According to 1 Corinthians 1:30, he will be able to escape all those things that will come to pass, and will be able to stand before the Son of man. In himself, our *God is a consuming fire* (Hebrews 12:29), and man out of Christ is merely as stubble, chaff, thorns, briars, and fuel for the wrath of this holy and sinner-consuming God to seize upon forever (2 Samuel 23:6-7; Isaiah 27:4; Malachi 4:1; Matthew 3:12; Hebrews 6:8). *Who can stand before his indignation? And who can abide the fierceness of his anger? His fury is poured out like fire, and the rocks are thrown down by him* (Nahum 1:6).

Now when these three books are opened, there will undoubtedly be sad throbbing and stinging in the heart of every person who stands for his life before the judgment seat of Christ, the righteous Judge. Without question, they will be studying a thousand ways to avoid and block the strike that, by the sin that these three books charge them with, will immediately fall upon them.

But now to dismiss all these at once, the witnesses immediately appear, and they are ready to testify and make full and soul-killing proof of every charge against them.

First Witness

The first is God Himself. He says, *I will be a swift witness against the sorcerers, and against the adulterers, and against false swearers, and against those that oppress the hireling in his wages, the widow, and the fatherless, and that turn aside the stranger from his right, and fear not me, saith the LORD of hosts* (Malachi 3:5).

The fact that God would now come in must necessarily have much impact with every soul. God says, "I will testify that these things of which you are accused before the Judge are true. I have seen all, know all, and wrote down all. There has not been a thought in your heart, nor a word on your tongue, that I have not thoroughly known about. All things have always been open and naked to My eye [Hebrews 4:13]. Yes, my eyelids try the children of men [Psalm 11:4]. I have known when you sit down and when you stand up, and I have understood your thoughts afar off. I have compassed your path, and am well acquainted with all your ways [Psalm 139:1-3]."

1. You have not continued in that state of nature in which I at first created you (Ecclesiastes 7:29). You did not want to retain that knowledge and understanding of God that you had, and could have had, by the very book of the creatures (Romans 1). You gave way to the suggestions of fallen angels, and so your foolish hearts were darkened and alienated and estranged from God (Romans 1:21).

2. All the creatures that were in the world have even condemned you. They have been fruitful, but you have been fruitless. They have been fearful of danger, but you have been foolhardy. They have taken the best opportunity for their own preservation, but you have both blindly and confidently gone on to your punishment (Proverbs 22:3).

3. Regarding the book of My remembrance, who can contradict it? *Do not I fill heaven and earth? saith the* Lord (Jeremiah 23:24). Was I not in all places to behold, to see, and to observe you in all your ways? My eye saw the thief and the adulterer, and I heard every lie and profanity of the wicked. I saw the hypocrisy of the pretender. *They have committed villany in Israel, and have committed adultery with their neighbours' wives, and have spoken lying words in my name, which I have not commanded them; even I know, and am a witness, saith the* Lord (Jeremiah 29:23).

4. God will also come in against them for transgressing His law, even the law that He delivered on Mount Sinai. He will open every part of the law in such order and truth, and will apply the offense of each particular person with such convincing argument, that they will fall down silenced forever. *Every mouth [will] be stopped, and all the world [will] become guilty before God* (Romans 3:19).

Second Witness

There is still another witness for condemning the transgressors of these laws, and that is conscience. *Their conscience also bearing witness*, said the apostle Paul (Romans 2:15). Conscience is a thousand witnesses. Conscience will cry "Amen" to every word that the great God speaks against you. Conscience is a forbidding accuser. It will keep pace with the witness of God as to the truth of evidence to a hair's breadth.

The witness of conscience is of great authority. It commands guilt and fastens it on every soul that it accuses. That is why it is said, *If our heart [or conscience] condemn us . . .* (1 John 3:20). Conscience will thunder and bring lightning at this day. Even the consciences of the most pagan sinners in the world will have sufficient reason to accuse, to condemn, and to make their faces drain of color, and *breaking of [their] loins* (Ezekiel 21:6), by reason of the force of its conviction. Oh, the mire and dirt that a guilty conscience, when it is forced to speak, will bring up and reveal before the judgment seat! It must speak out. No one can speak peace or health to that person upon whom God has let loose his own conscience.

Cain will cry, *My punishment is greater than I can bear* (Genesis 4:13); Judas will hang himself (Matthew 27:5); and both Belshazzar and Felix will feel the joints of their loins loosened and their knees smite one against another when conscience stirs (Daniel 5:6; Acts 24:25). Once conscience is thoroughly awakened, as it will be before the judgment seat, then God needs to say no more to the sinner than Solomon said to filthy Shimei: *Thou knowest all the wickedness which thine heart is privy to* (1 Kings 2:44).

This is as if to say, "Your conscience knows, and can well inform you of all the evil and sin that you are guilty of." As quickly as God brings forth the accusations, conscience answers to all the charges, even as face answers to face in a mirror, or as an echo answers the man who speaks, and cries out, "Guilty, guilty! Lord, I am guilty of all, of every part. I remember clearly all the crimes You lay before me." Thus, conscience will be a witness against the soul in the day of God.

Third Witness

As God and conscience will on this day be most dreadful witnesses against the sinful person, so also will those many thoughts that have passed through man's heart also be a witness against him. As Paul said before, *Their conscience also bearing witness, and their thoughts the meanwhile accusing or else excusing one another; in the day when God shall judge the secrets of men by Jesus Christ according to my gospel* (Romans 2:15-16).

The thoughts come in as a witness for God against the sinner upon the account of that unsteadiness and variety that were in them, both regarding God and their own selves. Sometimes the person thinks there is no God, but that everything has happened on its own, or by chance or fortune. *The fool hath said in his heart, There is no God* (Psalm 14:1; 53:1).

> People think that because they can sin with delight, that therefore God can let them escape without punishment.

Sometimes they think there is a God, but they think and imagine of Him falsely. *Thou thoughtest that I was altogether such an one as thyself*, God says, *but I will reprove thee* (Psalm 50:21).

People think that because they can sin with delight, that therefore God can let them escape without punishment. They often think that God either completely forgets their wickedness, or else that He will be pleased with such payment that they are pleased to give Him, even if it is only a few howling prayers (Hosea 7:14) or pretended and hypocritical tears and lamenting, which come from them more out of fear of the punishment of hellfire than because they have offended such a holy, just, and glorious God, and such a loving and humble Jesus (Malachi 2:13).

Sometimes people have had proper thoughts about something of God, but not about Him at the same time. They either think about His justice in such a way as to drive them from Him, which also causes them to put Him out of their mind (Job 21:14), or else they think only about His mercy and entirely forget about His holiness and justice. These are both simply corrupt thoughts about God, and are erroneous and sinful thoughts.

Sometimes people have somewhat accurate thoughts of God in regard to justice and mercy, but then, through the wretchedness of their unsatisfied nature and against this light and knowledge, they, with shut eyes and hardened hearts, rush fiercely, knowingly, and willingly again into their sins and wickedness (Hebrews 6:4-6; 10:26; 2 Peter 2:20).

Just as people have these various thoughts of God, so also their thoughts are not dependable about themselves. Sometimes they think they are sinners, and therefore they have need of mercy. Sometimes they think they are righteous, and so do not have as much need of mercy. Both of these thoughts are similarly debased and corrupt. The last is entirely senseless, and the first is not at all savingly sensible (Mark 10:17-22; Luke 18:11-12).

Sometimes people even think they are gods (Ezekiel 28:1-6), that they will never die, or that if they do die, they will never rise again (1 Corinthians 15:12) – or that if they do rise again, that they will be saved, even though they have lived wickedly and in their sins all the days of their lives (Deuteronomy 29:18-20). God will bring up every one of these thoughts, with ten thousand more that are similar in nature, against the rebels in the judgment day. Every one of these thoughts will be brought forth in their distinct order. He declares *unto man what is his thought* (Amos 4:13). *I know that thou canst do every thing, and that no thought can be withholden from thee* (Job 42:2).

We read that when the strangers at Jerusalem simply heard the apostles speak to everyone in their own language, it amazed and confounded them (Acts 2:6-8). However, how much more will they look and be amazed when God will evidently, clearly, and fully tell them all that was ever in their hearts, as well as every thought they have ever had!

The reason and strength of this witness will be that God will, by the manner and resentment that their thoughts had one to another, and by the contradiction that was in them, prove them to be sinners and ungodly. This is because sometimes they thought there was a God, and sometimes they thought there was none. Sometimes they thought that He was one type of God, and sometimes they thought of Him quite contrary. Sometimes they thought He was worth regarding, and sometimes they thought He was not. Sometimes they thought He would be faithful to mercy and justice and sinners, and sometimes they thought He would not be.

> They will appear to be a mass of sin, and a bundle of ignorance, of atheism, of unbelief, and of all things that would make them offensive to the judgments of God.

What greater argument can there be to prove that these people are vanity, empty, a lie, sinners, deluded by the devil, and those who have had false perceptions of God and His ways, His Word, His justice, and His holiness – and of themselves, their sins, and every action?

They will indeed appear to be a very lump of confusion, a mass of sin, and a bundle of ignorance, of atheism, of unbelief, and of all things that would make them offensive to the judgments of God. By calling up the thoughts of man; by showing them *that every imagination of the thoughts of [their] heart was only evil continually* (Genesis 6:5); and by showing them what shocking, drunken, wild, and vile thoughts they have had, both of Him and of themselves, God will convince them, declare them, and condemn them as sinners and transgressors against the book of creatures, the book of His remembrance, and the book of the law. By the manner of their thoughts, they will be proved to be unstable, ignorant, *wandering stars* (Jude 1:13), *clouds that are carried with a tempest* (2 Peter 2:17), without order or guidance, and taken captive by the devil at his will (2 Timothy 2:26).

While the wicked are standing trial for their lives before the judgment seat, and are doing so in the view of heaven and hell, hearing and seeing such dreadful things, both written and witnessed against every one of them, and that by such books and such witnesses that not only talk, but also testify with the whole strength of truth against them – they will then begin, though poorly, and without any benefit, to plead for themselves. Their plea will be somewhat like this:

Lord, we found in the Scriptures that You sent a Savior into the world to deliver us from these sins and miseries. We heard that this Savior also declared and openly offered Himself to such poor sinners as we are. Lord, Lord, we also made profession of this Savior, and many of us often took part in His holy ordinances. We have eaten and drunk in Your presence, and You have taught in our streets. Lord, some of us have also been preachers ourselves. We have prophesied in Your name, and in Your name we have cast out demons, and have done many wondrous works. Yes, Lord, we gathered among Your people. We forsook the profane and wicked world, and we carried our shining lamps before us in the face of all people. *Lord, Lord, open to us.* [Matthew 7:21-23; 25:1-2, 10-11; Luke 13:24-28]

The entire time they are pleading and speaking for themselves, see how earnestly they groan, how dreadful they look, and how the salty tears flow down like rivers from their eyes, as they intensify their petition, "Lord, Lord, Lord, Lord" – first thinking of this thing, and then of that, ever contending, seeking, and striving to enter in at this narrow gate. As Christ said, *When once the master of the house is risen up* (Luke 13:25) – that is, when Christ has laid aside His mediation for sinners and has taken upon Himself only to judge and condemn – then will the wicked begin to stand without and will knock and strive for a portion among those who are the blessed.

Oh, how their hearts will flutter while they look upon the kingdom of glory! How they will ache and throb at every view of hell, their proper place, as they continue to cry out, "Oh, that we might inherit life, and oh, that we might escape eternal death!"

The Book of Life

To take away all criticisms and objections of this nature that will arise in the hearts of these people, the book of life will be immediately brought out for a conclusion and a final end of eternal judgment. As John says, *The books were opened; and another book was opened, which is the book of life: and the dead were judged out of those things which were written in the books, according to their works* (Revelation 20:12).

But this book of life is not opened at this time because there are not any godly to be tried, for as I have shown before, their judgment is past and over before the wicked rise. The book of life, then, is now opened for further conviction of condemned reprobates so that their mouths may be stopped forever (Romans 3:19; Titus 1:11) in regard to their criticism, disputes, and arguments against God's proceeding in judgment with them. You can believe it that while God is judging them, they will resort to judging Him again, but He will be justified in His sayings, and will overcome when He is judged at this day (Romans 3:4).

Yet He will not overcome by hastily and angrily casting them aside, but by presenting a legal and convincing case against them. He will overthrow all their criticisms by His manifest and invincible truth. Wherefore, to prevent all that they can say, He will now open the book of life before them and will show them what is written in it in regard to election, conversion, and a truly gospel conduct and life. He will convince them that they are not of the number of His elect, they were never regenerate, and they never truly had a truly gospel conduct and life in the world.

By these three things, then, out of this book, you who are not saved must at last be judged and overcome.

1. You will be tried here to determine whether you are within that part of this book wherein all the elect are recorded, for all the elect are written here. As Christ said, *Rejoice, because your names are written in heaven* (Luke 10:20). As He said to His Father, *In thy book all my members were written* (Psalm 139:16; Hebrews 12:22-23).

Now, then, if your name is not found among the prophets, apostles, or the rest of the saints, you must be rejected as one who is cast away, as one polluted, and as *an abominable branch* (Isaiah 14:19). Your name is not found in the genealogies and rolls of heaven (Ezra 2:62). You have not been recorded as a recipient of everlasting life. Therefore, you will not be delivered from that soul-shocking misery, for even though they would give a thousand worlds, there is no soul that can be delivered on the day of God except those who are found written in this book. Every one of those who are written in this book, though not one of those who are not written, will in that day be delivered from the wrath to come (Daniel 12:1).

I think with what careful hearts the condemned will now begin to look for their names in this book. Those who, when the long-suffering of God once waited on them, made light of all His admonition and rejected the counsel of making their calling and election sure (2 Peter 1:10), would now give thousands of treasures if they could only see their names, even though it would be last and least among the sons of God.

But how they will fail, how they will faint, how they will die and languish in their souls when they will look and still see their names missing! How difficult it will be for Cain to see his brother recorded there, and he himself left out. Absalom will now faint and will be as one who gives up the ghost when he will see David his father and Solomon his brother written here, while he, however, is written in the earth among the damned. Sadness will be added to sadness in the soul of the perishing world when they fail to find their names in this part of *the book of life of the Lamb slain from the foundation of the world* (Revelation 13:8).

2. The second part of this book is that in which is recorded the nature of conversion, faith, love, etc. Those who have not had the authoritative and powerful Word of God upon them, and the true and saving operation of grace in their hearts (which is indeed the true life that is begun in every Christian), will be found still not written in this book – for the living, the holy living souls, are the only ones whose names are written therein. As the prophet Isaiah said, *He that remaineth in Jerusalem shall be called holy, even every one that is written among the living in Jerusalem* (Isaiah 4:3).

Eternal life is already in this life, begun in every soul that will be saved. As Christ said, *He that believeth in me hath everlasting life* (John 6:47), and *Whoso eateth my flesh, and drinketh my blood, hath eternal life; and I will raise him up at the last day* (John 6:54). This is why those who are written in this book are called the living. Here then, the Lord will open before you what conversion is, in the true and simple nature of it, which when you observe, you will then be convinced that you have missed true conversion in your life. It must necessarily be that when you observe by the records of heaven what a change, what a turn, what an alteration the work of regeneration makes on every soul and in every heart where the effectual call, or the call according to His purpose is (Romans 8:28), that you who have lived as a stranger to this, or have contented yourself with the idea only, or with a formal and artificial profession thereof, that it cannot be otherwise than that you must immediately fall down and conclude with grief that you have no share in this part of the book of life, but only the living are written in this book.

There is not one dead, carnal, wicked person recorded here. No. When the Lord will on this day make mention of Rahab, Babylon, Philistia, and Ethiopia – that is, of all the cursed masses and crew of the condemned – then He will say that this man was born there, that he was among them, and so has his name where they have theirs – under the black rod, in the King's black book, where He has recorded all His enemies and traitors. It will be said of this man, of this ungodly man, that he was born there (Psalm 87:4), that he lived and died in the state of nature, and so lived and died under the curse of God, even as others. As God said of wicked Coniah, *Write ye this man childless* (Jeremiah 22:30), so He says of every ungodly person that so departs out of this world, "Write this person graceless."

Wherefore, among the Babylonians and Philistines, among the unbelieving Moors and pagans, his name will be found in the day when it will be inquired where every person was born, for on this day, God will divide the whole world into two groups: the children of the world and the children of Zion. The honor, the privilege, and the advantage that the godly will have above the wicked at the day when they give an account to God, when the Lord makes mention of Zion, will be that it will then be acknowledged that this and that (good) person was born there. *The LORD shall count, when he writeth up the people, that this man was born there* (Psalm 87:6). This person had the work of conversion, of faith, and of grace in his soul. This person is a child of Zion, of the heavenly Jerusalem, whose name is also *written in heaven* (Galatians 4:26; Hebrews 12:23). Blessed are the people who are in such a situation (Psalm 144:15).

But, poor soul, counterfeit coins will not pass for gold now. While you judged yourself by the twisted rule of your own reason, ideas, and desires, you were pure in your own eyes; but now you must be judged alone by the words and rule of the Lord Jesus. His word will not now, as previously, be squeezed and twisted this way and that to comfort you in your hypocrite's hope and carnal confidence; but even if you are a king or emperor, no matter who you are, the word of Christ, and that with this interpretation only, will judge you in the last day (John 12:48).

Sinners will then begin to cry with loud and bitter cries, "Oh, I would give ten thousand worlds for a saving work of grace. I would give crowns and kingdoms for the smallest amount of saving faith, and for the love that Christ will say is the love of His own Spirit."

Sinners will then also begin to see the work of a broken and contrite spirit (Psalm 51:17) and of walking with God as living stones in this world (1 Peter 2:5). Sadly, though, these things appear in the hearts of the condemned too late, as also everything else does. This will be only like the repentance of the thief around whose neck is the rope, for the unfortunate circumstance of the condemned will be that the glory of heavenly things will not appear to them until it is too late.

Christ will then indeed be shown to them, as also will be the true nature of faith and all grace, but it will be when the door is shut and mercy is gone. They will pray and repent most earnestly, but it will be in the time of great waters of the floods of eternal wrath, when they cannot come near Him (Psalm 32:6; Matthew 25:10-12; 1 Timothy 6:15).

Tell me, then, sinner, if Christ would now come to judge the world, can you endure the trial of the book of life? Are you confident that your profession of faith, your conversion, your faith, and all other graces you think you have will prove to be gold, silver, and precious stones on that day? Behold, He comes as a refiner's fire and as fuller's soap (Malachi 3:2). Will you indeed be able to endure the melting and washing of this day? Examine beforehand, and test yourself sincerely, for everyone *that doeth truth cometh to the light, that his deeds may be made manifest, that they are wrought in God* (John 3:21).

You say you are a Christian and that you have repented, that you believe and love the Lord Jesus, but the question is whether these things will be found of equal length, height, and breadth with the book of life, or whether, when you are weighed in the balance, you will yet be found lacking (Daniel 5:27). How will it be if, when you come to speak for yourself before God, you would say *Sibboleth* instead of *Shibboleth* – that although almost, yet you do not properly and naturally know and speak the language of the Christians (Judges 12:6)?

If you miss only one letter in your testimony, you are gone, for although you may deceive your own heart with brass instead of gold, and with tin instead of silver, yet God will not be so deceived (Galatians 6:7). You know how confident the foolish virgins were, and yet they were deceived. They gathered with the saints, they went forth from the foul pollutions of the world, they each had shining lamps, and they all went forth to meet the bridegroom, yet they missed the kingdom. They were not written among the living at Jerusalem. They did not have the true, powerful, saving work of conversion, of faith, and of grace in their souls. Those who are foolish take their lamps, but they take no oil, no saving grace, with them (Matthew 25:1-4).

So you see how it will be with sinners before the judgment seat from these two parts of this book of life.

3. However, there is still another part of this book to be opened, and that is the part in which are recorded those noble and Christian acts that they have done since the time of their conversion and turning to Christ. Here are recorded the testimony of the saints against sin and antichrist, their suffering for the sake of God, their love to the members of Christ, their patience under the cross, their faithful frequenting the assemblies of the saints, and their encouraging one another to stay strong in His ways in the worst of times, even when the proud were called happy and when those who worked wickedness were praised. As the Scriptures say, *Then they that feared the LORD spake often one to another: and the LORD hearkened, and heard it, and a book of remembrance was written before him for them that feared the LORD, and that thought upon his name* (Malachi 3:16).

For indeed, as truly as any person has his name found in the first part of this book of life, and his conversion in the second, so there is a third part, in which his noble, spiritual, and holy actions are recorded and written down. As it was said by the Spirit to John about those who suffered martyrdom for the truth of Jesus, *Write, Blessed are the dead which die in the Lord from henceforth: Yea, saith the Spirit, that they may rest from their labours; and their works do follow them* (Revelation 14:13).

The labors of the saints and the book of life are mentioned together, signifying that the travels, labors, and acts of the godly are recorded therein (Philippians 4:3).

The Lord tells Sardis that those among them who endured

to the last gasp in the faith and love of the gospel would not be blotted out of the book of life. Rather, they, with the work of God on their soul and their labor for God in this world, would be confessed before His Father and before His angels (Revelation 3:5).

This part of this book is in another place called *the book of the wars of the* LORD (Numbers 21:14) because in it are recorded these famous acts of the saints against the world, the flesh, and the devil.

You find also how exact the Holy Spirit is in recording the travels, efforts, labor, and goodness of any of the children of Israel in their journey from Egypt to Canaan, which was a representation of the travels of the saints from nature to grace and from grace to glory. King Ahasuerus kept in his library a book of records in which was written the good service that his subjects did for him at any time. This was also a type of the manner and order of heaven.

Just as Mordecai, when search was made, was found in the book of records to have done such and such service for the king and his kingdom (Esther 6:1-2), so certainly will it be found at the day of inquiry what every saint has done for God. You find in the Old Testament also, when any of the kings of Judah died, that there was surely a record in the book of Chronicles of their memorable acts and doings for their God, the church, and the commonwealth of Israel, which still further shows unto the children of men that all the kings of the New Testament, who are the saints of God, have all their acts and what they have done for their God recorded in the book of Chronicles in the heavenly Jerusalem.

When this part of the book of life will be opened, what can be found in it of the good deeds and heaven-born actions of wicked men? Simply nothing, for as it is not to be expected that thorns would bring forth grapes, or that thistles would bear figs

(Matthew 7:16), so it cannot be imagined that ungodly people would have anything of their honor recorded in this part of the book of life.

What have you done, man, for God in this world? Are you one of those who have set yourself, like Job and Paul (Job 1:8; 2 Corinthians 10:4-5), against those strong struggles of pride, lust, covetousness, and secret wickedness that remain in your heart? Do your struggles against these things arise from pure love to the Lord Jesus, or from some terrors of the law and conviction for sin (Galatians 5:6)? Do you struggle against your lusts because you truly love the sweet, holy, and blessed leading of the Spirit of the Lord Jesus and His leading you into His blood and death for your justification and deliverance from wrath to come (2 Corinthians 5:14; Philippians 3:6-8)?

What acts of self-denial have you done for the name of the Lord Jesus among the sons of men? What house, what friend, what wife, what children, etc. have you lost or left for the Word of God and the testimony of His truth in the world? (Matthew 19:27-29; Revelation 12:11)? Were you one of those who sigh and afflict yourself for the abominations of the times, and whom Christ has marked and recorded as such a person (Ezekiel 9:4; Zephaniah 3:18)?

> What acts of self-denial have you done for the name of the Lord Jesus among the sons of men?

In a word, are you one of those who would not be won, either by fear, frowns, or flatteries, to forsake the ways of God or wrong your conscience? Are you one of those who reject those opportunities that Satan and this world often give you to return to sin in secret (Hebrews 11:15)? These are the people whose praise is in the gospel and whose commendable and worthy acts are recorded before the Judge of all the world.

Sadly, these things are strange to a carnal and wicked person. He has done nothing like this in this life, and therefore, how can any such things be recorded for him in the book of life? He must necessarily be shut out of this part also. As David said, *Let them be blotted out of the book of the living, and not be written with the righteous* (Psalm 69:28).

The wicked will find nothing for their comfort in the first part of this book, where all the names of the elect are, nor will they find anything for their comfort in the second part of the book, where are recorded the true nature and operation of effectual conversion, faith, love, or similar things. The wicked will also not find anything in this third part, in which are recorded the worthy acts and memorable deeds of the saints of the Lord Jesus.

Therefore, when Christ has opened before them this book of life and has proven out of it on that day that the ungodly one is wrong, He will then close the book and say, "I find nothing in this book that will do you any good. You are not of My elect. You are a son of perdition." For as these things will be found clear and full in the book of life, so they will be found powerfully worked in the hearts of the elect, all whose conversion and perseverance will then be opened before your eyes as a witness of the truth of what you see opened before you, and also of your unregenerate condition.

> Now the saints are hidden, but then they will be unmistakable. This is the day in which the Lord will show who are His.

You will then see what a turn, what a change, and what a clinging to God, to Christ, and to His Word and His ways there was found in the souls of the saved ones! You will also see how resolutely, sincerely, and wholeheartedly the true child of God opposed, resisted, and warred against his most dear and cherished lusts and corruptions.

Now the saints are hidden, but then they will be unmistakable. This is the day in which the Lord will show who are

126

His. He will show who fear the Lord and who do not fear Him (Psalm 83:3; 1 Samuel 8:19; Numbers 16:5; Malachi 3:18). You will see how Abraham left his country (Hebrews 11:8), how good Lot stayed close to God in profane and wicked Sodom (2 Peter 2:7-8), how the apostles left all to follow Jesus Christ (Matthew 19:29); and how patiently they endured all crosses, afflictions, persecutions, and necessities for the kingdom of heaven's sake. You will see how they endured burning, striving, stoning, hanging, and a thousand calamities, and how they manifested their love to their Lord, His cause, and His people in the worst of times and in the days when they were most rejected, insulted, abused, and abased.

> *Then shall the King say to them on his right hand* [and will do so when all the devils and condemned sinners stand by], *Come, ye blessed of my Father, inherit the kingdom prepared for you from the foundation of the world* [you are indeed the truly converted souls, as appears by the grace that was in your hearts]: *for I was an hungered, and ye gave me meat: I was thirsty, and ye gave me drink: I was a stranger, and ye took me in: naked, and ye clothed me: I was sick, and ye visited me: I was in prison, and ye came unto me.* (Matthew 25:34-36)

"You confessed Me, stood by Me, and denied yourselves to nourish Me and My poor members in our low, weak, and most despised condition."

The world will see, hear, and be witnesses of this against themselves and their souls forever, for how can it be otherwise than that these poor condemned sinners would be forced to confess that they were both without Christ and without grace when they will be shown, both in the book of life and in the hearts of the holy and beloved souls, that which they are quite empty of and greatest strangers to?

By the fruits of regeneration, the saints, even in this world, testify to the world not only the truth of conversion in themselves, but also that those who are not converted are without Christ, and so are without heaven and without salvation (1 Thessalonians 2:10; 1 Timothy 6:12; 2 Timothy 2:2). Sadly, while we are here, they will resist this testimony of our happiness by calling our faith fiction, our communion with God delusion, and the sincere profession of His Word before the world hypocrisy, pride, and arrogance. Yet when they see us on the right hand of Christ, joined with the angels of light, and themselves on His left hand, joined with the angels of darkness; and when they will see our hearts and ways opened before their eyes, and acknowledged by the Judge for honest hearts and good ways – those same ways that they hated, mocked, rejected, and despised – what will they say, or what can they say, except this: "We fools considered their lives to be absurdity, and their end to be without honor; but how they are numbered with the saints and acknowledged by God and Christ!"

Truly, if it were not that the world might be convinced of the evil of their ways, or be left without more excuse in the day of God (along with some other reasons) by seeing the change that is worked in the godly at their conversion, I am convinced that they would not stay away from heaven as long as they do, nor undergo so much abuse and hardship as frequently befalls them.

By extending the life of His people who are scattered here and there among men in this world, God is making work for the day of judgment and the overthrow of the hard-hearted forever and ever; and, as I have said, by the conversion, life, patience, self-denial, and heavenly mindedness of His dear children, this will give them a heavy and most dreadful blow.

When God has thus laid open the work of grace, both by

the book of life and the Christian's heart, then their pleading what gifts and abilities they had in this world will of itself fall to the ground. They will then see that gifts and grace are two separate things. They will also see that whosoever is without grace, no matter how excellent their gifts are, must perish and be lost forever. Despite all their gifts, they will be found to be workers of iniquity, and will so be judged and condemned (Matthew 7:22-23).

That is a notable place in the prophecy of Ezekiel: *Thus saith the Lord GOD; If the prince* [the Prince of Life] *give a gift to any of his sons* [that is, to any who are truly gracious], *the inheritance* [or the profit that he gets thereby] *shall be his sons'* [that is, for the exercise of his gift he will receive a reward]; *it shall be their possession by inheritance. But if he give a gift of his inheritance to one of his servants* [who is not a son], *then it shall be his* [but only] *to the year of liberty; after, it shall return to the prince* (Ezekiel 46:16-17).

This day of liberty is when the Judge sits upon the throne for judgment, even the glorious *liberty of the children of God* (Romans 8:21), when Christ will then say to those who stand near, *Take from him the pound, and give it to him that hath ten pounds. This servant must not abide in the house for ever, though with the son it shall be so* (Luke 19:24; see also John 8:35). A man may be used as a servant in the church of God, and may have many gifts and much knowledge of the things of heaven, yet end up being no more than a very bubble and nothing (1 Corinthians 13:1-3).

But on that day, they will clearly see the difference between gifts and grace, even as clearly as those who have eyes can now see the difference between gifts and ignorance, and very foolishness. This day does indeed abound with gifts. Many bright minds are seen in every corner. People have the Word of God and truths of Christ at their fingers' ends, but sadly, with many, yes, a great many, there is nothing but knowledge and gifts; they are only words. All their religion lies in their tongues and heads. The power of what they say and know is seen in others, but not in themselves. These are like the lord on whom the king of Israel leaned: they will see the plenty, the blessed plenty that God provides and will bestow upon His church, but they will not taste of it (2 Kings 7:17-20).

Observations

First, before I conclude this matter, observe that among all the objections and criticisms that are made, and will be made, by the ungodly in the day of the Lord Jesus, they have not one complaint about election and reprobation. They do not murmur at all that they were not predestined to eternal life. The reason for this is because then they will see (though now they are blind) that God could in His royal prerogative, without prejudice to those who are damned, choose and refuse at pleasure. Besides, at that day they will be convinced that there was so much reality and absolute willingness in God, in every offer of grace and mercy to the worst of people, and also so much goodness, justness, and reasonableness in every command of the gospel of grace (which they were so often entreated and urged to embrace), that they will be drowned in the conviction that they refused love, grace, reason, etc. for hatred, they refused grace for sin, and they refused things reasonable for things unreasonable and vain.

They will then see that they left glory for shame, God for the devil, heaven for hell, and light for darkness. They will see that even though they made themselves beasts, God made them reasonable creatures, and that He, with reason, expected them to have adhered to and have delighted in things that are good and according to God's will and Word.

Yes, they will then see that although God did not determine to bring them to heaven against their hearts and wills and the love that they had for their sins, they will be convinced that God was far from infusing anything into their souls that would in the least hinder, weaken, obstruct, or prevent them from seeking the welfare of their souls.

People will now talk and babble at a fast pace about election and reprobation, and they will conclude that because all are not elected, therefore God is to blame that any are damned. However, they will then see that they are not damned because they were not elected, but because they sinned. They will also see that they did not sin because God put any weakness into their souls, but because they gave in willingly, knowingly, and fully to Satan and his suggestions, and so turned away *from the holy commandment delivered unto them* (2 Peter 2:21). They will then see that although God at times fastened His cords around their heads, heels, and hands, both by godly education and sharp convictions, yet they fervently rushed away from it all, saying, *Let us break their bands asunder, and cast away their cords from us* (Psalm 2:3). God will be justified in His sayings, and clear when He judges (Psalm 51:4), even though your proud ignorance wants to have, and to multiply, complaints and arguments against Him.

> The ungodly will then see that they are not damned because they were not elected, but because they sinned.

Secondly, as the whole body of the elect, by the nature of conversion in their hearts, will witness a non-conversion in the hearts of the wicked, and as the ungodly will fall under the conviction of this cloud of witnesses, so, to increase their conviction, there will also be opened before them all the labors of the godly, both ministers and others, and the efforts that they have taken to save, if it had been possible, these condemned wretches. It will then come burning hot upon their souls how often they were forewarned of this day. They will then see that there was never any trial or day of judgment more publicly foretold of than this day.

You know that before the judges begin their trials, they declare that they take heed to the laws and statutes of the king of the country. Rebel – you will this day be convicted that every sermon you have heard and every serious debate you have been at about the things of God and the laws of eternity were to you as the judge's declaration before the trials and judgment began. Every exhortation of every minister of God is as that which Paul gave to Timothy and commanded him to give in charge to others: *I charge thee before God, and the Lord Jesus Christ, and the elect angels, that thou observe these things* (1 Timothy 5:21), and again, *I give thee charge in the sight of God, who quickeneth all things, and before Jesus Christ, who before Pontius Pilate witnessed a good confession; that thou keep this commandment without spot, unrebukable, until the appearing of our Lord Jesus Christ* (1 Timothy 6:13-14).

Paul gave these instructions, he said, that they may be blameless. You have heard and seen this, yet you have not held fast to it. Instead, you have cast away the things that you have heard and have been warned of. Sadly, God will multiply His witnesses against you.

1. Your own vows and promises will be a witness against you that, contrary to your light and knowledge, you have destroyed your soul, as Joshua said to the children of Israel when they said the Lord should be their God. Joshua said to the people, *Ye are witnesses against yourselves that ye have chosen you the LORD, to serve him.* That is, Joshua said that if they turn back again, even this covenant and resolution of theirs will on the great day be a witness against them. *And they said, We are witnesses* (Joshua 24:22).

2. Every time you have spoken well of godliness, and then continued in wickedness; or every time you have condemned sin in others, while not refraining from it yourselves – every such word and judgment that has passed out of your mouth, sinner, will be as a witness against you on the day of God and of the Lord Jesus Christ. As Christ said, *By thy words thou shalt be justified, and by thy words thou shalt be condemned* (Matthew 12:37).

I observe that no matter who you talk with, they will say that serving God, loving Christ, and walking in ways of holiness are best, and that the best will come from this. I also observe that people who are blatantly wicked themselves will still, with harsh rebukes and judgments, condemn drunkenness, lying, covetousness, pride, and immorality, along with all manner of abominations in others. In the meantime, though, they continue to neglect God and embrace sin and the temptations of the flesh themselves.

Every time such people speak well of godliness and then continue in their sins, they pass judgment upon themselves and provide a witness, even their own mouth, against their own soul at the judgment seat. Christ said, *Out of thine own mouth will I judge thee, thou wicked servant* (Luke 19:22). "You knew what I was, and that I loved to see all My servants zealous and active for Me so that at My coming I might have received again what I gave you, with increase. Therefore, you should have been busying yourself in My work for My glory and for your own good. However, since you have acted contrary to this against your own light and mouth: Angels, take this unprofitable servant and cast him into utter darkness. There will be weeping and gnashing of teeth. He sinned against his light, and he will go to hell against his will" (Matthew 25:26-31).

The very same result will befall all those who have used their mouths to condemn the sins of others while they themselves live in their sins. God says, "Oh, you wicked wretch, you knew that sin was bad. You condemned it in others. You also condemned and passed judgment upon them for their sin." *Therefore thou art inexcusable, O man, whosoever thou art that judgest* (for you who judge do the same thing). Therefore, *wherein thou hast judged another, thou condemnest thyself* (Romans 2:1).

Therefore, Christ says that He must look upon you to be nothing other but a sinner against your own mouth, and cannot judge you as anything less than one who despises His goodness, and the riches of His forbearance. In doing so, you have treasured up *wrath against the day of wrath and revelation of the righteous judgment of God* (Romans 2:1-5). He who *knoweth to do good, and doeth it not, to him it is sin* (James 4:17). God will accordingly judge and condemn poor sinners, even from and by themselves, to the fire, that lake of brimstone and fire.

3. God has said in His Word that rather than there being a lack of witness at the day of judgment against the workers of iniquity, the very dust of their city that clings to His messengers who publish the gospel will itself be a witness against them. That is why Christ said to His disciples, *Into whatsoever city ye enter, and they receive you not, go your ways out into the streets of the*

same, and say, Even the very dust of your city, which cleaveth on us, we do wipe off against you. . . . But I say unto you, that it shall be more tolerable for Sodom, than for that city at the judgment (Luke 10:10-12).

It may be that when you hear that the dust of the street (that clings to a minister of the gospel while you reject his word of salvation) will be a witness against you at the day of judgment, you will be apt to laugh and say, "The dust a witness! Witnesses will be scarce where dust is forced to come in to plead against someone." Well, sinner, do not mock. *God hath chosen the foolish things of the world to confound the wise; and God hath chosen the weak things of the world to confound the things which are mighty* (1 Corinthians 1:27).

How do you speak? If God had said by a prophet to Pharaoh, only two years before the plague, that He would soon come against him with one army of lice, a second army of frogs, a third army of locusts, etc., and would destroy his land, do you think it would have been wise of Pharaoh to have laughed such a message to scorn? Is anything too hard for the Lord? Has He said it, and will He not bring it to pass? (Jeremiah 32:27; Numbers 23:19; Isaiah 14:24). You will see in the day of judgment what strength all these things will have as witnesses against the ungodly.

I could call many more witnesses up, but at this time these are sufficient to be named, for *in the mouth of two or three witnesses shall every word be established* (2 Corinthians 13:1). *At the mouth of two witnesses, or three witnesses, shall he that is worthy of death be put to death* (Deuteronomy 17:6; John 8:17).

With the books being opened, the laws read, the witnesses heard, and the ungodly convicted, the Lord and Judge then proceeds to the sentence and punishment of the wicked.

The Sentence and Punishment of the Wicked

The sentence of eternal death passes upon the wicked: *Depart from me, ye cursed, into everlasting fire, prepared for the devil and his angels* (Matthew 25:41). The Judge continues: "By the book of the creatures, by the book of God's remembrance, by the book of the law, and by the book of life, you are now judged guilty of high treason against God and Me, and as murderers of your own souls, as these faithful and true witnesses here have testified, every one of them appearing in their most upright testimony against you. Also, you never had a saving work of conversion. You never had true faith. You died in your sins. Neither can I find anything in the last part of this book that will help you. No worthy act is here recorded of you. When I was hungry, you did not give Me any food. When I was thirsty, you did not give Me anything to drink. When I was a stranger, you did not take Me in. When I was naked, you did not clothe Me. I was sick and in prison, but you did not visit Me [Matthew 25:42-43]. I have made a thorough search among the records of the living, and I find nothing of you or of your deeds written therein. *Depart from me, ye cursed, into everlasting fire, prepared for the devil and his angels.*"

Thus will these poor ungodly creatures be stripped of all hope and comfort, and therefore will fall into great sadness and wailing before the Judge. Yes, they will cry out, as being reluctant to let go, yet to no avail. Even as the person who has fallen into the river will grab hold of anything when he is struggling for his life, even though it tends to hold him more firmly under the water to drown him, so, while these poor creatures, as they lie struggling and writhing under the angry countenance of the Judge, will bring out yet one more faint and weak groan – and there goes life and all. Their last sigh is this: "Lord, when did we see You hungry and gave You no food? When did we see You thirsty and gave You nothing to drink? When did we see You a stranger and did not take You in? When did we see You naked and did not clothe You? When were You sick or in prison, and we did not minister unto You?" (Matthew 25:44).

You see how unwilling the sinner is now to accept a "no" of everlasting life. He who once could not be persuaded to reconcile with the Lord Jesus, even though one would have persuaded him with tears of blood – see how closely he now remains near the Lord, what arguments he makes with mournful groans, how with excuses and words he seeks to gain time and delay the execution: "Lord, open unto us! *Lord, Lord, open to us!*" (Matthew 25:11).

"Lord, You have taught in our streets, and we have taught in Your name. In Your name we have cast out demons. We have eaten and drunk in Your presence. When did we see You hungry, or thirsty, or a stranger, or naked, or sick, or in prison and did not minister to You?" (Matthew 7:22; Matthew 25:37-39; Luke 13:26).

Oh, poor hearts! How reluctantly and unwillingly they turn away from Christ! How hesitant they are to partake of the fruit of their ungodly doings! Christ must tell them to depart once, and then again, before they will depart. After He has shut the door upon them, they continue to knock and cry out, *Lord, open unto us.* After He has given them their answer that He does not know them, they still plead and mourn. Therefore, He is ready to answer again: *I tell you, I know you not whence you are; depart* (Luke 13:25-27).

Depart. Oh, this word: *depart*! How dreadful it is! With what weight it will fall on the head of every condemned sinner! You must note that while the ungodly stand before the Judge, they have a most clear view both of the kingdom of heaven and of the condemned souls in hell. They see the God of glory, the King of glory, the saints of glory, and the angels of glory, as well as the kingdom in which they have their eternal abode. They also begin to see the worth of Christ and what it means to be smiled upon by Him. They must depart from all this.

Just as they will have the view of this, so will they most clearly behold the pit, the bottomless pit, the fire, the brimstone, and the flaming beds that justice has prepared for them of old (Jude 1:4). Their acquaintances will also be very conspicuous and clear before their watery eyes. They will now see who and which ones are wicked and condemned souls. Their great-grandfather Cain and all his children, with Judas and his companions, will be their fellow agonizers in the flames and pain forever. Oh, what a grievous day! What a grievous word!

This word "depart" therefore looks two ways and commands the condemned to do so also. Depart from heaven, and depart to hell. Depart from life, and depart to death. *Depart from Me*: now their eternal fate is sealed indeed.

The Savior turns them away and casts them down. God has given Him authority to execute judgment also *because he is the Son of man* (John 5:27). *Depart from Me*: "I came to do you good, but you rejected Me." Now then, although you desire it ever so willingly, yet you shall not have it.

Depart from me, ye cursed. You lie open to the stroke of justice for your sins. You have been forsaken and left of God, you vessels of wrath, you despisers of God and goodness, and you must now have vengeance feed on you, for when you were in the world, you fed on sin. You treasured up wrath against this day of *wrath and revelation of the righteous judgment of God* (Romans 2:5).

Depart from me, ye cursed, into everlasting fire. Fire is that which of all things is the most unbearable and unendurable. The agonizing state of the ungodly after judgment is shown by fire. Who can eat fire, drink fire, and lie down in the midst of flames of fire? Yet the wicked must do this. This is not only fire, but it is everlasting fire. *Behold, how great a fire a little matter kindleth!* (James 3:5). A little sin, a little pleasure, a little unjust dealing and doing – what preparation is made for the punishment of these sins!

Therefore, the fire into which the condemned fall is called the lake, or sea, of fire: *And whosoever was not found written in the book of life was cast into the lake of fire* (Revelation 20:15). Little did the sinner seriously think that when he was sinning against God, he was making such provision for his poor soul; but now it is too late to repent. His worm will never die, and his fire will never be quenched (Mark 9:48). Although the time in which people commit sin is short, yet the time of God's punishing them for their sin is long.

Depart from me, ye cursed, into everlasting fire, prepared for the devil and his angels. By saying *prepared for the devil and his angels,* He implies a further conviction upon the consciences of the condemned. It is as if He had said, "As for this fire and lake that you must go to, although you did not think much about it because you were careless, yet I did occasionally put you in mind of what the fruits of sin would be – even by preparing this judgment for the devil and his angels. In his creation, the devil is far more noble than you, yet when he sinned, I did not spare him. He sinned also before man did, and after he sinned, I cast him down from heaven to hell and hung the chains of everlasting darkness upon him [Jude 1:6], which might and should have rightly caused you to take heed, but you would not [Genesis 3:2-5]."

Wherefore, since you have sinned as he has done, and you did so after he had both sinned and was bound over to eternal punishment, the same justice that lays hold on these more noble creatures must surely lay hold on you (Revelation 20:1). The world should be convinced of judgment, then, *because the prince of this world is judged* (John 16:11). This should happen before they come to this condition of hearing the eternal sentence rattle in their ears, but since they did not regard it then, they must and will feel the sting of it now. *Depart from me, ye cursed, into everlasting fire, prepared for the devil and his angels.*

> God wants people to learn what both mercy and justice is to them by showing mercy and justice to others.

God wants people to learn what both mercy and justice is to them by showing mercy and justice to others, but if people are foolish and careless in the day of patience, they must learn by suffering in the day of rebukes and vengeance. This is how it was with the old world. God gave them one hundred and twenty years' warning by the preparation of Noah for the flood that would come, but since they then were careless and would not consider the works of the Lord nor His warning them by this preparation, therefore He brought in the flood upon the world of the ungodly, as He here brings the last judgment upon the workers of iniquity and sweeps them all away in their willful ignorance (Matthew 24:37-39).

Wherefore, by these words: *prepared for the devil and his angels*, the Lord Chief Judge as good as says, "This fire into which now I send you did of itself, even in the preparation of it (if you had considered it), forewarn you of this that now is come upon you. Hellfire is not a new or unheard-of thing. You cannot now plead that you have never before heard of it, nor could you with any reason think that since I prepared it for angels – for noble, powerful, and mighty angels – that you, poor dust and ashes, would escape the vengeance."

Depart from me, ye cursed, into everlasting fire, prepared for the devil and his angels. The sentence being thus passed and the work of judgment being complete, it remains now for everyone to go to his eternal location. Wherefore, this mighty company, with heavy heart, now promptly returns from before the judgment seat, and that with great speed, God knows, for their rightful destination is the hell of hell, into which they descend like a stone into a well, or like Pharaoh into the bottom of the Red Sea (Exodus 15:10). With all hope being now taken from them, they must necessarily fall with intensity into the jaws of eternal desperation, which will deal far worse with the souls of men, and will make a greater slaughter in their tortured consciences, than the lions in the den with Daniel could possibly have done with the men who were cast in among them (Daniel 6:24).

This is that which Paul calls *eternal judgment* (Hebrews 6:2), because it is that which is last and final. Many are the judgments that God executes among the sons of men, some after this manner and some after that. Many of these continue for some time, but none of them are eternal. The longest and most terrible of all the judgments of God is the very demons and condemned spirits in hell, yet they must pass under another judgment, even this last, great, and final judgment. *The angels which kept not their first estate, but left their own habitation, he hath reserved in everlasting chains under darkness unto the judgment of the great day* (Jude 1:6).

It is the same in regard to condemned souls, for both Sodom and Gomorrah, with all others, although already in hell in their souls, must still, as I have shown before, all arise to this judgment, which will be their final judgment. Other judgments of God have an end, so the end of many of them prove to benefit those on whom they are inflicted, being God's instrument of conversion to sinners. This may be appropriately compared to those lesser judgments among men, such as putting them in the stocks, whipping them, or burning them in the hand. Such punishments and judgments often prove profitable to those who are punished with them.

Eternal judgment, however, is more comparable to those more severe judgments among men, such as beheading, shooting to death, hanging, and drawing and quartering, which gather up all, even health, time, and the like, and cut off all opportunity of good, leaving no place for mercy or correction. *These shall go away into everlasting punishment* (Matthew 25:46). *Depart from me, ye cursed, into everlasting fire, prepared for the devil and his angels.* This is the last word the condemned are likely to hear forever. It is the last voice they will hear, and therefore it will stick longest and with most power on their slaughtered souls. There is no rescinding or negating these words. This is the very windup of eternal judgment.

The judgment then being over, the kingdom ceases to be any longer in the hand of the man Christ Jesus, for as the judges here among men, after they have travelled their judicial circuit then deliver up their commission to the king, so Christ the Judge now delivers up His kingdom to His Father, and now all is swallowed up in eternity. The condemned are swallowed up in eternal justice and wrath, and the saved are swallowed up in eternal life and bliss. The Son also delivers up the kingdom to the Father and subjects Himself under Him who did put all things under Him so *that God may be all in all* (1 Corinthians 15:24-28).

For now the end is come, and not before – even the end of the reign of death itself. Death, hell, sinners, and demons must now fall together into the lake that burns *with fire and brimstone* (Revelation 20:14-15; 21:8). Now is the end of Christ's reign as the Son of man, and the end of the reign of the saints with Him in this, His kingdom, which He has received from His Father for His work's sake, which He did for His Father and for His elect. The apostle Paul wrote, *Then cometh the end, when he shall have delivered up the kingdom to God, even the Father.* But when will that be? He answers by saying:

> *When he shall have put down all rule and all authority and power. For he must reign, till he hath put all enemies under his feet. This will not be until the final sentences and judgment are over, for the last enemy that shall be destroyed is death. For [God] hath put all things under his feet. But when he saith all things are put under him, it is manifest that he is excepted which did put all things under him. And when all things shall be subdued unto him, then shall the Son also himself be subject unto him that put all things under him, that God may be all in all.* (1 Corinthians 15:24-28)

Conclusion

With all things being now at this stage, everyone being in his proper place – God in His, Christ in His, the saint in his, and the sinner in his – I will conclude with this brief note upon both the state of the good and the bad after this eternal judgment.

The righteous then will never fear death, the devil, and hell ever again, and the wicked will never have hope of life. The just will forever have the victory over these things, but the wicked will everlastingly be swallowed up by them.

The holy will be in everlasting light, but the sinners will be in everlasting darkness. The sinners will be without light, yet in fire always burning, yet not consumed. They will always be afraid of death and hell, frantically desiring to be annihilated to nothing. They will continually fear to stay long in hell, yet will be absolutely sure that they will never leave it. They will forever desire the saints' happiness, yet will always envy their bliss. They want to have it because it is easy and comfortable, yet they cannot stand to think of it because they have lost it forever. They are forever burdened with the delight of sin, yet that is the greatest torture: they are always desiring to put it out of their mind, yet they unquestionably know they must forever endure the guilt and torment thereof.

The saints are always enlivened with the consideration of the grace that they have embraced, but the wicked are most intensely tormented with the thoughts of rejecting and refusing it. The just, when they think of their sins, are comforted with the thoughts of being delivered from them; but when the ungodly think of their righteousness, they will consume themselves to think that this would not deliver them from hell. When the godly think of hell, it will increase their comfort; but when the wicked think of heaven, it will bite them like a serpent.

Oh, this eternal judgment! What would a condemned soul give that there might be an end put to this eternal judgment, even after thousands and hundreds of thousands of millions of years! But their misery is that they have sinned against a God who is eternal. They have offended that justice that will never be satisfied, and therefore they must endure the fire that will never be quenched (Mark 9:48). This is judgment, just and sad.

As it is with good and bad in general, the wicked, who are judged and condemned and receive sentence of the fiery gulf, will find more specifically that just as when he who busies himself to do good will have more glory than others, so those who have been more busy and active in sin than others will have more wrath and torment than others. For as doing abundant good enlarges the heart to receive and hold more glory, so doing abundant evil enlarges the heart and soul to receive more punishment.

That is why there are such sayings as these: *It shall be more tolerable in that day for Sodom, than for [others]* (Luke 10:12) – that is, it will be more tolerable than for those who had sinned against much greater light and mercy. These people *shall receive greater damnation* (Luke 20:47). Yes, it stands to reason that he who had the most light, the most conviction, the most means of conversion, and who was the highest toward heaven must necessarily have the greatest fall and so will sink deepest into the jaws of eternal misery.

> For as doing abundant good enlarges the heart to receive and hold more glory, so doing abundant evil enlarges the heart and soul to receive more punishment.

As one star – that is, as one saint – differs from another in heaven (1 Corinthians 15:41), so one condemned soul will differ from another in hell. It is so among the demons themselves; some are worse than others. Beelzebub is the chief, or *prince of the devils* (Matthew 9:34; Mark 3:22). That is, he was one who was most glorious in heaven, a leader among the reprobate angels before his fall (Isaiah 14:12). Therefore, he sinned against the greater light, mercy, and goodness, and so became the leader for wickedness, and will also have the leading torments as the wages thereof.

What is prayed for against Babylon will be true of the damned in hell: *How much she hath glorified herself, and lived deliciously, so much torment and sorrow give her* (Revelation 18:7). Can it be imagined that Judas, who betrayed the Prince of life and Savior of the world, would have no more torment than others who never came near his wickedness by ten thousand degrees? He who knew his master's will and did not prepare himself, nor did according to his will, will be *beaten with many stripes* (Luke 12:47) – with many more stripes than others who through ignorance committed sin worthy of many stripes (Luke 12:48).

But what should I say about the degrees of the torments of the condemned souls in hell? All will suffer, for he who suffers least, will the waters of a full cup be wrung out to him? The least measure of wrath will be the wrath of God – eternal and fiery wrath, unbearable wrath. It will lay the soul in the gulf of that second death, which will forever have the mastery over the poor condemned, perishing sinner.

> *And death and hell were cast into the lake of fire.*
> *This is the second death.*
> *And whosoever was not found written in the book of*
> *life was cast into the lake of fire.*
> —Revelation 20:14-15

About the Author

John Bunyan was born in November 1628, in Elstow, England. A celebrated English minister and preacher, he wrote The Pilgrim's Progress (1678), the book that was the most characteristic expression of the Puritan religious outlook. His other works include doctrinal and controversial writings; a spiritual autobiography, Grace Abounding (1666); and the allegory, The Holy War (1682).

Other Similar Titles

Pilgrim's Progress, by John Bunyan

Often disguised as something that would help him, evil accompanies Christian on his journey to the Celestial City. As you walk with him, you'll begin to identify today's many religious pitfalls. These are presented by men such as Pliable, who turns back at the Slough of Despond; and Ignorance, who believes he's a true follower of Christ when he's really only trusting in himself. Each character represented in this allegory is intentionally and profoundly accurate in its depiction of what we see all around us, and unfortunately, what we too often see in ourselves. But while Christian is injured and nearly killed, he eventually prevails to the end. So can you.

The best part of this book is the Bible verses added to the text. The original *Pilgrims Progress* listed the Bible verse references, but the verses themselves are so impactful when tied to the scenes in this allegory, that they are now included within the text of this book. The text is tweaked just enough to make it readable today, for the young and the old. Youngsters in particular will be drawn to the original illustrations included in this wonderful classic.

Available where books are sold.

The Holy War, by John Bunyan

What if you were able to see your life from a spiritual perspective and see the actual reality of the verse above? How does our enemy, Diabolus, plan and carry out his attacks? How do his demons help, and what are their objectives? Why and how must we petition Emmanuel to get His attention and help in this great, holy war?

Written four years after *The Pilgrim's Progress*, John Bunyan followed up with this second allegorical classic, which has touched hearts and minds of readers for generations. The epicenter of this book is the town of Mansoul, its people (such as Conscience, Self-Denial, and Do-Right), and its gates (Eye-gate, Ear-gate, Mouth-gate, Nose-gate, and Feel-gate). The attack by Diabolus and his demons, all of whom have appropriate names, is carefully planned and executed. As still happens to men today, Mansoul fell hard. Emmanuel is of course willing to help, but can only do so on special, seemingly strict terms. As you watch this intense battle unfold, you'll be emboldened to fight with new vigilance, to guard the gates with tenacity, and to rely on Emmanuel's sovereignty like never before.

Available where books are sold.

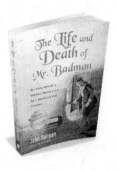

The Life and Death of Mr. Badman,
by John Bunyan

The life of Mr. Badman forms a third part to *The Pilgrim's Progress*, but it is not a delightful pilgrimage to heaven. On the contrary, it is a wretched downward journey to the infernal realms. The author's goal is to warn poor, thoughtless sinners, not with smooth words they can ignore, but with words that thunder against their consciences regarding the danger of their souls and the increasing wretchedness into which they are madly hurrying. The one who is in imminent but unseen danger will bless the warning voice if it reaches his ears, however rough and startling it may sound.

The life of Badman was written in an age when abandonment of moral principles, vice, gluttony, intemperance, habitual lewdness, and the excessive unlawful indulgence of lust marched like a ravaging army through our land, headed by the king, along with officers from his polluted peers. Is this book not also written for today, then?

Available where books are sold.